the police officer and criminal justice

RELATED BOOKS

Sullivan, John L.: INTRODUCTION TO POLICE SCIENCE
Stuckey, Gilbert B.: EVIDENCE FOR THE LAW ENFORCEMENT OFFICER

the police officer and criminal justice

R. Gene Wright
Director of Law Enforcement and Corrections
Cabrillo College

John A. Marlo
A.B., J.D.
Attorney at Law

McGraw-Hill Book Company
New York   St. Louis   San Francisco   Düsseldorf
London   Mexico   Panama   Sydney   Toronto

the police officer and criminal justice

Copyright © 1970 by McGraw-Hill, Inc. All rights reserved. Printed in the United States of America. No part of this publication may be reproduced, stored in a retrieval system, or transmitted, in any form or by any means, electronic, mechanical, photocopying, recording, or otherwise, without the prior written permission of the publisher.

Library of Congress Catalog Card Number 77-104741

07-072097-5

5 6 7 8 9 0 VBVB 7 9 8 7 6 5

This book was set in Janson by Vail-Ballou Press, Inc., and printed on permanent paper and bound by Vail-Ballou Press, Inc. The designer was Richard Paul Kluga; the drawings were done by John Cordes, J. & R. Technical Services, Inc. The editors were Cary F. Baker, Jr., and Joseph F. Murphy. Sally R. Ellyson supervised the production.

preface

Historically the police officer and the criminal justice system have operated as separate entities, coming together only at the apex of a criminal case and separating again during the post-trial procedures. This operational system, though not altogether ineffective, has resulted in some rather wide gaps of understanding and philosophy regarding justice as an American institution. Today we see the emerging roles in the entire system of criminal justice developing a closer relationship and demanding that such gaps be narrowed through more cooperative efforts from arrest to release of all suspected criminal offenders.

It is unreasonable at this point in evolution to expect that all practitioners in the criminal justice occupational area will or can be equally educated or professionally developed to the same degree of sophistication or expertise in all areas of concern. It is not unreasonable, however, to expect that all practitioners have equal appreciation and basic understanding of the fundamental concepts and philosophies of the system.

We think it especially important that the police officer of today be thoroughly acquainted with the criminal procedure responsibilities of the entire court system and be able to identify his role in this system.

R. Gene Wright
John A. Marlo

contents

preface v

chapter 1. a brief historical review   1

Some Points from the Past   *1*
Historic Development   *2*
   The Code of Hammurabi   *3*
   Greek Contributions   *4*
   Roman Contributions   *4*
   French Contributions   *5*
   English Contributions   *5*
   The Magna Carta   *7*
   Colonial Development   *7*
   A Look to the Future   *8*

chapter 2. the establishment of courts of law   13

What Is a Court?   *13*

Authority for the Establishment of Court
Systems   15
   The United States Constitution   *15*
   The California State Constitution   *16*
   The Electorate   *16*
How and Why Courts are Established   17
Court Systems   19
   Civil and Criminal Proceedings Compared   *19*
   Degree of Proof   *20*
   Code of Civil Procedure   *20*
Criminal Proceedings   21
   Nature of Criminal Proceedings   *21*
Trial Systems   22
   Court Trial   *22*
   Jury Trial   *22*
The American Jury System   23
Kinds of Juries   23
General Aspects of Jurors and Juries   24

chapter 3.   court organization and administration   27

The Federal Court System   27
   The United States Supreme Court   *28*
   The United States Circuit Court of Appeals   *29*
   The District Courts of the United States   *29*
   Separate Federal Courts   *30*
Jurisdiction   30
   Concurrent Federal and State Jurisdiction in Some Criminal Matters   *30*
The State Court System   31
   State Supreme Court   *31*
   Intermediate Court of Appeals   *31*
   Local Courts of General Jurisdiction   *32*
   Local Courts of Limited Jurisdiction   *32*
   Municipal Courts   *32*
The California Court System   32
   The California State Supreme Court   *33*

        District Courts of Appeal   34
        Superior Courts   35
        Municipal Courts   37
        Justice Courts   37
        The Grand Jury   38
        Court Sessions   44
    Officers of the Courts   45
        Clerks   45
        Attorneys at Law   45
        Bailiffs   46
        Judges   46
        Magistrates   47
    The Judicial Council   47

chapter 4.   accusatory pleadings and arraignments   51

    The Pleading   51
        Information, Indictment, and Complaint   52
        Rules of Pleading   53
    Arraignments   54
        Presence of Defendant   55
        Procedure at Arraignment   55
        Time to Plead   57
        Pleas   57
        Right to Counsel   58
    Statute of Limitations   59
        Defined   59
        Specific Crimes   60
        When Prosecution Barred   60
        Defendant Out of State   61
        Lesser Included Offenses   61

chapter 5.   post-plea and pretrial proceedings   65

    Setting the Cause   65
        Automatic Dismissal   66

Waiver of Time   66
Insanity   66
    Procedure Once Insanity Plea Is Entered   66
    Procedure When Insanity Plea and Not-guilty
    Plea Are Entered   67
    Burden of Proof   67
    Test for Insanity   67
Present Insanity   68
    During the Trial   68
    Before Execution   69
Change of Venue   69
    Court's Discretion   70
    Trial Publicity   70
Continuances   70
Dismissals   71
    Misdemeanor Actions   71
    Superior Court Actions   72
    Dismissal on Court's Own Motion
    or by the District Attorney   73

chapter 6.   preliminary examinations   75

Purpose   75
Plea of Guilty   76
Waiver of Preliminary Examination   76
The Examination   77
    Procedure: Time to Prepare   77
    Postponement   77
    Reading of Witnesses' Depositions   77
    Presence of Defendant   77
    Examination of Defendant   78
    Examination of Witnesses   78
    Exclusion and Separation of Witnesses   78
    Exclusion of the Public   79
Discharge   79
"Sufficient Cause"   80
Held to Answer   81
Commitment   81

chapter 7. the trial 83

Order of Trial 83
Qualifications of Jurors 84
Selection of the Jury 85
Types of Challenges 86
  Challenges for Cause 86
  Judge's Decision as to Bias 90
Peremptory Challenge 91
Swearing in of the Jury 92
Trial Procedure 92
  The Prosecutor's Role 92
  The Defense Counsel's Role 95
  The Public Defender 97
  Opening Statement 99
  Objections 99
  Presentation of Evidence 100
  Final Argument 102
  Instructions to the Jury 104
  Deliberation 107
The Verdict 108
  General Verdict 109
  Special Verdict 109
  Degree 109
  Previous Offenses 109
  Two or More Defendants 110
  Lesser Offenses and Attempts 110
  Recommendations and Correction of the Verdict 110
  Recommendation of Sentencing 110

chapter 8. post-trial proceedings 113

Post-trial and Prejudgment Procedure 113
  Referral to Probation Officer 115
  Hearings and Determinations on Motions for a New Trial 115
  Question of Insanity and Commitment to a Diagnostic Facility 115

Motions for a New Trial and in
Arrest of Judgment   *116*
Sexual Psychopath Proceedings   *120*

chapter 9.   judgment and sentence   135

Presence of Defendant   *135*
Indeterminate Sentences   *138*
Degrees of Crime   *138*
Concurrent and Consecutive Sentencing   *140*
  Habitual Criminal   *141*
The Death Sentence   *144*

chapter 10.   probation   149

The Basic Law of Probation   *149*
Application for Probation   *153*
Conditions of Probation   *154*

chapter 11.   proper court presentation and testimony   159

The Police Officer's Role in Court   *159*
The Importance of Appearance, Manner, Demeanor, and Speech   *161*
Preparation for Court   *164*
Presentation of Evidence   *166*
Use of Notes   *166*

chapter 12.   laws of arrest   169

Arrest with Warrant   *169*
  The Warrant   *170*
  Execution of Service   *171*
  Out-of-town Warrants, Teletypes, Bulletins, etc.   *174*
Arrest without a Warrant   *175*
  Arrest by Peace Officers   *175*

Arrest by Private Citizens 179
The Doctrine of Reasonable Cause 180
Duties during and after Arrest 182
Defendant's Right to Counsel 184
Defendant's Right to Remain Silent 185
The Legal Admonishment 185
Confessions 186
Evidence 186
Extradition 187
Arrest with a Warrant 187
Arrest without a Warrant 188
Waiver of Extradition 189
Extradition to California from Another State 189
The Right to Bail 189
Upon Arrest 190
After Preliminary Examination 191
Nonbailable Offenses 192
Bail Proceedings 192
Dismissal 192
Conviction 193
Arrest by Surety 193
Forfeiture 193
Release on Own Recognizance 193

chapter 13. writs, motions, and appeals   197

Writ of Coram Nobis 197
Motion to Set Aside Judgment 198
Motions Subsequent to Judgment 198
Motion for New Trial 198
Effect of Granting New Trials 199
Procedure 199
Demurrer 199
Appeals by the Defendant 201
The Appellate Courts 201
The Supreme Court 201
District Court of Appeal 201

    Superior Court *201*
   Procedure *202*
    Appeals from Inferior Courts *202*
    Appeals from Superior Courts *202*
    Appeals by the People *202*
    Appealable Conditions *203*
    Bail *203*
   Dismissals *204*
    Voluntary *204*
    Involuntary *204*
   Habeas Corpus *205*
    Jurisdiction *205*
    Illegal Restraint *206*
    Unlawful Restraint under Legal Detentions *206*
    Petition *207*
    Form and Contents of Application *207*
    Service of Copy of Application *207*
    Direction *208*
    Return *208*
    Body Produced *209*
    Exceptions *209*
    Hearing *209*
    Discharge or Removal to Custody *210*

glossary *213*

index *219*

1

a brief historical review

American law enforcement is literally a part of the American court system. No other profession outside the structure of the system itself is so desperately dependent upon it for day-to-day guidance and support. The modern professional police officer must recognize the court as an essential vehicle in the administration of justice. The courts are the only public agencies ultimately responsible for both safeguarding our constitutional rights as citizens and providing restraints that ensure the reasonable safety and welfare of our country and its people. Individually and collectively, citizen and policeman alike depend more upon the judgment of the various courts than either likely realizes. Thus it becomes an absolute necessity that a firm understanding of our administration of justice be widely shared in the field of professional law enforcement.

SOME POINTS FROM THE PAST

It is likely that several thousand years ago a caveman, clad in his best prehistoric tiger skin, stood before his peers and sadly related how he had been relieved of his *Tyrannosaurus* "T" bones by a thieving member of the community. In his day and in his society, complexity was not a problem. His needs were simple, and his life was geared to the very basic drives that kept him alive.

As a result of his simplicity, however, the caveman's meager food supply was among the most important and valuable of possessions. The foul burglary of his prehistoric pantry was therefore upsetting to his clan as well as to himself. After an investigation had revealed the identity of the criminal the victim undoubtedly was brought to a kind of trial by his clansmen. It is unlikely that a lawful arrest using "sufficient force" was made, nor are chances good that search-and-seizure rules were closely followed. A smudge of grease on the defendant's mouth might well have been prima facie evidence of his guilt, and the criminal court procedure applied was very likely a brief hearing to decide which would be the most amusing method of implementing the death sentence.

It is difficult for us to envision such a social structure, even though it actually survived for many thousands of years without a formal system of governmental regulation. By comparison civilization, the system to which we have become so accustomed and take so much for granted, is brand-new. We have but scratched the surface in the determination of democratic justice processes, and, if we remain attentive, the next few hundred years should teach us a great deal.

HISTORIC DEVELOPMENT

We can trace some dubious systems of administering justice as far back as 2,000 years before the birth of Christ. Historians tell us that crude retributive practices were utilized in the Assyrian empire (Nineveh). It is not likely that the Assyrians tempered justice with the "milk of human kindness," as they were well known for their merciless practices as warriors. In fact, the concept of justice as it is known today is a relatively new turn in the history of jurisprudence.

The Code of Hammurabi. Hammurabi, King of the Babylonians in the 1900s B.C., is credited with recognizing that a society functions more uniformly when governed by a set of standard rules. Highly sophisticated for its day, the Code of Hammurabi was nonetheless founded on the concept of *lex talionis*, "an eye for an eye." For example, it stipulated: "If a man destroy the eye of another man, they shall destroy his eye." Implicit obedience of a father was demanded from children, for we read: "If a son strike his father, they shall cut off his fingers." Medical quacks and corrupt building contractors were punished in the following way: "If a physician operate on a man for a severe wound with a bronze lancet and cause the man's death; or open an abcess [in the eye] of a man . . . and destroy the man's eye, they shall cut off his fingers." And again: "If a builder build a house for a man and do not make its construction firm, and the house which he has built collapse and cause the death of the owner of the house, that builder shall be put to death."

But while punishments were stern, the code, on the whole, attempted to secure a crude form of justice. Punishments were graded in their severity so that the higher the culprit in the social scale, the more severe the penalty. The status of women was fairly high, but the code largely was designed for a man's world. The following clause refers to an erring wife: "If she has not been economical, but a gadder-about, has neglected her house and belittled her husband, they shall throw that woman into the street." *

The code shows that punishment for offenses had been removed from the hands of the clan and family and placed within the administrative responsibilities of the government.† About 400 years later a system of courts and judges developed by the Egyptian government encompassed responsibility for punishing corruption and bribery.

* Quotations from Hammurabic Code are taken from Robert Francis Harper, *The Code of Hammurabi*, The University of Chicago Press, Chicago, 1904.
† T. Walter Wallbank and Alastair M. Taylor, *Civilization Past and Present*, Scott, Foresman and Company, Glenview, Ill., 1949, p. 76.

It is significant in the history of the administration of justice that Moses, in about 1200 B.C., set down ten principles of good behavior that have been included in one form or another in almost every code of laws put into effect since that time. These rules of conduct were known as the Law of Moses, or the Ten Commandments.

Greek Contributions. Solon, archon of Athens in 594 B.C., revolutionized law into a less drastic form of control and developed the administration of justice into a more or less democratic tool of government. The Greeks were among the first to realize that laws are man-made and not a direct ultimatum from a divine source. As a result, law became more elastic to the needs of society. If laws were man-made, it was accepted that they could also be man-changed, a completely new thought in legal philosophy.

The Greeks respected law more than any people had before. They believed that a country should be ruled by law rather than by individual personalities. Greek governmental officials were likely the first to be carefully limited in their power by law, and the philosophy of administering laws "to the spirit" was introduced.

Solon's proposals were a great step forward in the development of law in that he persuaded the Athenian nobles to treat all citizens alike in matters of justice. A famous record of Greek jurisprudence is Plato's *The Laws*. Plato, the great Greek philosopher, saw far ahead and recognized that punishment by law should not be retributive in nature but rather an instrument of correction and rehabilitation.

Roman Contributions. Although the Greeks were the first to recognize formal codified law, the ancient Romans were the first to develop and sophisticate it. A committee was sent from Rome to study the work of Solon and other Greek lawmakers and produced, in 449 B.C., the Law of the Twelve Tables. These tables, inscribed on brass tablets, were codified rules of behavior based primarily on the Roman religion. Rome instituted the position of "praetor," a forerunner of the modern judge. The praetors were responsible for administering justice under the Law of the Twelve Tables but were also authorized to make legal decisions regarding cases not covered by codified law.

A great step in the development of law was the codification or classification of Roman laws by the emperor Justinian. Roman jurists had for some time been working to bring all the laws together in logical, written form so they might be presented to the world in a unified and organized grouping. Justinian's Digest and Code fulfilled this desire and ultimately had a great influence on the development and philosophy of later European laws.

Seneca, a Roman statesman (4 B.C.–A.D. 65), philosophized that "punishment is designed to protect society by removing the offender, to reform its subjects, and to render others more obedient." * It would seem that the philosophy of law had reached a high sophistication that almost equalled present-day practices. Unfortunately, however, the following 500 years found Europe in a state of war, destruction, and decline. As formal law and an organized, stable government are interdependent, little was accomplished during this period. In fact, many of the earlier sophistications were buried with the societies that formulated them.

French Contributions. In A.D. 785, the Capitularies of Charlemagne were issued in France. This was a complicated set of laws dealing with weights and measures, tools, sales, burial of the dead, emergency procedures for famine and pestilence, and crime.†

English Contributions. About this same time, Anglo-Saxon England was beginning to emerge, but the English were obviously lacking in the sound philosophies of earlier Greek and Roman de-

---
* A. C. Germann, Frank D. Day, and Robert J. Gallati, *Introduction to Law Enforcement*, Charles C Thomas, Publisher, Springfield, Ill., 1963, p. 38.
† *Ibid.*, p. 40.

velopment. The most vivid examples of early Anglo-Saxon law were the three classic methods of trial or guilt determination: (1) trial by ordeal, (2) trial by combat, and (3) trial by compurgation.

In proving his innocence through "trial by ordeal" the defendant was required to undergo physical tests. If he could place his arm into a vat of boiling oil, walk barefoot across a bed of burning coals, or drink a potion of deadly poison—all without the usual result of physical harm—he was considered not guilty. In some jurisdictions the defendant's arm was immersed in the boiling oil and he was placed in a cell for several days. The cell undoubtedly was dirty, rat-infested, and without sunlight. After a proper interlude he was removed from the cell and his arm was examined. If it had healed normally, he was considered to have been found not guilty. If, however, the arm had become infected, it was deemed to be a sure sign of guilt, and the defendant was punished according to his crime.

"Trial by combat" was normally a method of determining which of two principals was justified in a mutual dispute. Here the two were pitted against each other in combat, the winner, naturally, being exonerated of all guilt.

"Trial by compurgation" was more sophisticated and far less dangerous. It required the accused to take a very serious oath and then to tell the truth regarding his alleged act. This was followed by the testimony of "compurgators," persons who would swear to the defendant's innocence.

It was England, after all, that developed the system of law upon which modern American jurisprudence is mainly based. A court system was developed, and "vicecomes," forerunners of the modern circuit judge, were introduced. Criminal law began to formalize itself, and crimes were classified as to seriousness and degree. In 1166 the jury system was born in the Assize of Clarendon. This, in effect, was the prototype of our grand jury concept. With these developments came the practice of recording the proceedings of law, which resulted in standardized procedures based on precedents set down by judges. Over a period of time these decisions came to be known as "common law" and are the basis for English and American law to this day.

The Magna Carta. Perhaps the most significant of all historical events in relation to modern American administration of justice occurred at Runnymede, England, on June 15, 1215. It was here that King John of England affixed his seal to the Magna Carta. The Magna Carta was written in Latin and its name is literally translated as "The Great Charter." The document is commonly called "the cornerstone of English liberty." Prior to the adoption of the Magna Carta, the English people had suffered many injustices at the hands of King John. Ironically it was not the people as such but rather the landowning barons who finally forced King John to sign the document. The long struggle between the barons and the high-tax–imposing kings culminated in this agreement, which was destined to become a foundation for democratic constitutional law in the United States of America. It was not until some years—and many amendments—later that the charter became final and guaranteed the rights as we understand them today. However, the charter marked the beginning of democracy in England and provided essentially for two kinds of rights: (1) the rights of the barons, as promised by the King, and (2) the rights of the freemen, as promised by the barons.

The charter's three most significant rights, upon which much constitutional law is based, were (1) the right to fair taxation, (2) the right to habeas corpus, and (3) the right to justice by means of a fair trial.

Colonial Development. The English common law was brought to North America by the colonists and is the basis for American law today. Some states still employ a common law principle in criminal actions, while California, like most, has developed a system of statutory law that simply reflects much of the common law philosophy.

Many changes, however, have been made in specific instances to bring the law more into keeping with the American way of life. For example, English law held that if a man's cattle were not fenced in and subsequently destroyed the crops of another, the owner of the cattle causing such destruction was liable for damages. This was a very practical law in England, where the land holdings were small and close together. In America, however, during the development of the Western frontier, cattle ranches were huge in size while farmlands were relatively small. In order to be fairly applied the law had to be completely reversed and required the farmer to fence in his crops if he wished protection from the cattle. If he did not take this precaution, he had no grounds for a legal action if an errant cow trampled his corn patch.

The American system of administering justice has today become an extremely complicated vehicle of jurisprudence. It is complicated, however, only in the sense of its own intricacies; it remains rather simple and uncluttered in its broad, general philosophies. The most vivid example is in the outward-appearing simplicity of the Bill of Rights, which has proposed so many extremely complicated questions of law.

A LOOK TO THE FUTURE

An introductory chapter to any work of practical knowledge would hardly be complete without a speculative look into the future. The general subject of law poses a large question mark for law enforcement with every new decision of the courts. As the attitudes and values of the country change, so will the courts be motivated in their administration of justice. That which is justice today may not be so termed tomorrow and may by the next day have taken on still another new meaning under the law. Modern police officials have learned to expect and accept these changes as part of our legal system and will comply readily or reluctantly, depending upon the effect of the decision. The pertinent question for law enforcement is: What must we do to adequately comply with the decisions of the courts?

It sometimes seems that the police are at the end of the proverbial rope, that legal hocus-pocus has tied their hands and made them ineffective—while the courts sit aloof, highly critical of police methods. Every police officer and official has experienced this feeling. Yet few have given up the fight to conduct police business in a highly professional manner and in direct compliance with the courts of law. This in itself is an extremely healthy sign and points brightly toward a future of firmer understanding of the mutually serious responsibilities.

When we unthinkingly complain that police "effectiveness" is being lost in legal entanglements, we should remind ourselves that the most "effective" police in our era were the Gestapo of Hitler's Germany and the Russian MVD (Secret Police). This kind of "effectiveness" is not compatible with the American system of justice. On the other hand, the courts themselves have a direct responsibility to recognize that the police are working under considerable limitations and fully deserve the support and confidence that the court is sometimes reluctant to bestow.

What the future will bring certainly cannot be revealed in this or any other study. Even educated predictions will not solve the problems until they are actually met on every front and under every condition. Preparation for the future, however, is a meaningful start, and preparation begins with understanding. The remainder of this book is devoted to fostering just such understanding in the field of criminal justice.

SUMMARY

The American court system has evolved from history and grown with society's needs and demands. The early historical attempts at controlling antisocial behavior were crude and retributive. The first known codified law was developed by the Babylonians in the 1900s B.C. and is known as the Code of Hammurabi.

Prior to the birth of Christ the Greeks and Romans developed social laws that held promise of high sophistication, but the turmoil of this time destroyed such efforts, which were buried with the societies that formulated them.

In A.D. 785, the French contributed the Capitularies of Charlemagne, which provided legal control of civil and criminal conditions as well as some aspects of health and safety.

In this same era, Anglo-Saxon England developed formal procedures of law. The first attempts were not as philosophically sophisticated as the earlier Greek and Roman contributions and were based on superstition and the doctrine of divine intercession. But it was England after all that developed the basis of law upon which modern American jurisprudence was essentially founded.

The most significant historical event affecting American law was the signing of the Magna Carta in 1215. From this legal breakthrough we have inherited such rights as the right to fair taxation, the right to habeas corpus, and the right to justice by means of a fair trial.

The English "common law," based on judicial decisions, was transported to colonial America, where accommodation to the particular American condition has resulted in most law becoming codified in accordance with various specific social interests.

DISCUSSION QUESTIONS

1. Describe the legal needs of a primitive society. What causes such needs to grow and demand a more sophisticated development?
2. Compare the Hammurabic Code with modern concepts of justice.
3. What common concepts in modern law can be found relative to the Law of Moses?
4. Compare the early Greek and Roman legal developments. Why did they fail?

5. Describe trial by ordeal, combat, and compurgation. What did they have in common?
6. Discuss the Magna Carta and equate its concepts with present-day legal philosophy.
7. How does the English common law affect American law? Compare the two kinds of law.
8. Discuss the dynamics of change that are taking place in American law today.

2

the establishment of courts of law

WHAT IS A COURT?

In the abstract sense a court is really many things to many people. It may be a haven of refuge to the oppressed, a ground on which a civil wrongdoing may be remedied, an authority by which existing laws can be interpreted, or a means of public protection through control of crime and criminals. To the law enforcement officer it is the last step in the investigation-prosecution process. Depending on his past experience, he may walk into court confident, unconfident, or somewhere in between. The truly effective officer feels he is a part of the court and strives to win its affection and support. By the same standard, the effective court feels that it is a part of law enforcement and strives to bring the collective responsibility along closer lines of understanding and productive attitude. It is well that neither the law enforcement officer nor the court become entangled in a web of narrow objectivity lest the individual and collective needs of the people whom they serve suffer even the smallest indignity or inattention.

In a material sense the American court is a judicial tribunal. Its main functions are to hear and pronounce judgment on all points of law that fall within its jurisdiction or authority. The court is set up in many systems and on all governmental levels (see Chapter 3). It is organized to administer law and legal processes and is itself established and governed by such law with a unique set of checks and balances designed to ensure each citizen his constitutional right to due process. It is made up mainly of judges, juries, attorneys, and witnesses and has, more than any other governmental body, retained a dignified image in the eyes of the people.

It is not so difficult to understand the American court system if we remember that all courts fall into one of two categories. They are either *federal courts,* which are run by the United States government, or *state courts,* which are conducted by each of the various states. The "jurisdiction," or the authority to hear certain cases, is set down by law and varies among the two systems. Federal courts, for example, have "exclusive jurisdiction" over (1) all civil actions in which the United States or a state is a party, except those between a state and its own citizens; (2) all cases involving crimes against the United States government; and (3) all admiralty maritime, patent-right, copyright, and bankruptcy cases arising under the United States Constitution or national statutes.

Similarly, the state courts enjoy "exclusive jurisdiction" over matters of primary concern to the state. Some of these types of cases are (1) civil disputes between individuals, and between individuals and state and local government; (2) trials of persons accused of violating the state's criminal laws; and (3) protection of constitutional rights of citizens against infringement by state or local authorities.

A third possibility in the question of jurisdiction is cases that fall in the "exclusive jurisdiction" of neither the federal court nor the state court. In such cases it is up to the initiating party to determine which court he prefers. And, of course, a case started in even the lowest state court can feasibly end up being heard in the highest federal court through the appellate system.

AUTHORITY FOR THE ESTABLISHMENT OF COURT SYSTEMS

The United States Constitution. The first established authority for our court systems, as in most governmental organizations, is found in the United States Constitution. Although it refers specifically to the federal courts, the Constitution provides a basis upon which most of state's judiciary systems are created. The specific legal authority is found in Article III, sections 1 and 2, which follow in their entirety:

ARTICLE III

Section 1. The judicial Power of the United States, shall be vested in one Supreme Court, and in such inferior Courts as the Congress may from time to time ordain and establish. The Judges, both of the supreme and inferior Courts, shall hold their Offices during good behaviour, and shall, at stated Times, receive for their Services a Compensation which shall not be diminished during their Continuance in Office.

Section 2. The judicial Power shall extend to all Cases, in Law and Equity, arising under this Constitution, the Laws of the United States, and Treaties made, or which shall be made, under their Authority;–to all Cases affecting Ambassadors, other public ministers and Consuls;–to all Cases of admiralty and maritime jurisdiction;–to Controversies to which the United States shall be a Party;–to Controversies between two or more States;–between a State and Citizens of another State;–between Citizens of different States;–between Citizens of the same State claiming lands under Grants of different States, and between a State, or the Citizens thereof, and foreign States, Citizens or Subjects.

In all Cases affecting Ambassadors, other public Ministers and Consuls, and those in which a State shall be Party, the supreme Court shall have original jurisdiction. In all the other

Cases before mentioned, the supreme Court shall have appellate jurisdiction, both as to Law and Fact, with such Exceptions, and under such Regulations as the Congress shall make.

The trial of all Crimes, except in Cases of Impeachment, shall be by jury; and such Trial shall be held in the State where the said Crimes shall have been committed; but when not committed within any State, the Trial shall be at such Place or Places as the Congress may by Law have directed.

The California State Constitution. It would be cumbersome and unrealistic to attempt to examine here the legal authorities of each state. It would also be incomplete if we looked at the state systems only in general terms. As an alternative, we shall define the general structure of most state systems and use the California system as a specific example. (Also see Chapter 3.)

The authority for the system of California courts is found in article VI, section 1, of the California Constitution, which reads as follows:

> The judicial power of this State is vested in the Supreme Court, courts of appeal, superior courts, municipal courts, and justice courts. All except justice courts are courts of record.

These powers are very general in nature. The mechanics of the organization and administration of the courts are spelled out in procedural laws, which are found or supplemented in such legal sources as the United States Administrative Code and the various codes of civil and criminal procedure. As our discussion becomes more specific the text will include many pertinent citations of such sources, to which the reader may refer for further study or clarification.

The Electorate. We usually find that the courts themselves are pretty well established and are little affected by the general electorate. However, in almost all cases judges and justices are elected officials, the main exceptions being United States federal court judges and justices, who are appointed by the President with the advice and consent of the Senate (see Chapter 3).

In California the electorate is responsible for the election of magistrates on all levels. Supreme Court justices are elected at the general election and hold office for a period of twelve years. District Court of Appeal justices are also elected for twelve-year terms, but by the voters in their respective districts. Superior Court judges are elected by the voters of their county and serve for terms of six years.

HOW AND WHY COURTS ARE ESTABLISHED

We have discussed some of the ways in which courts are established and the legal authorities which allow their establishment. Since the court systems are entirely creations of the various governments, we have only to refer to the proper legal documents for the authorizing clauses. There are, however, special provisions covering special conditions. For example, one of the duties of the chairman of the Judicial Council is, under certain conditions, to assign judges to assist courts with congested calendars or an as-yet-unfilled vacancy. Obviously, if there were no provisions to keep the courts in operation, even a small delay would cause insurmountable entanglements of calendars and permit something less than due process to the parties concerned.

It is not difficult to justify the reasons for having courts of law. History has shown us quite vividly that we can survive individually only when we live within the structure of organized government. This poses two basic alternatives of governmental formation. We may either have a democratic form of governmental organization or we may have a totalitarian form. Since we are definitely involved with the former, there is no need to pursue the question. Because a democratic form of government requires laws and standards, we must practice two further concepts in order to make it work. These are the concepts of "law enforcement" and "justice." Obviously, law enforcement by itself can easily become totalitarian unless justice is administered through some fair and impartial system. This is where courts enter the picture. They are the nucleus for the administration of justice.

When there is more than one person present in any one place, there will almost certainly be differences of opinion. When these differences become serious enough to endanger the well-being or dignity of an individual, he may rely on the court to resolve the matter through legal process. This is his right as a citizen and his duty as a member of the community. It is interesting to note that in almost every case of "rights of the citizen" there is also the question of individual responsibility, and this is a factor which can never be overshadowed or ignored if we are to achieve true justice for all persons.

Another reason for having courts is to provide an authority for the control of crime and criminals. This, of course, is of vital concern to the law enforcement officer. In recent years and months we have seen rapid and relatively drastic readjustments in the administration of American criminal justice. Many of the problems, real and imagined, that have arisen between the courts and law enforcement during this transition have yet to be resolved. It is enough to say here that the administration of criminal justice would be impossible without the dual efforts of both the courts and law enforcement. The responsibility of carrying out this process is one of today's most vital concerns.

The third and last basic reason (that we shall discuss here) for having courts is that the courts are designed to protect our liberties. Essentially we find most guarantees of liberties in the United States Constitution. The first ten amendments—known as the Bill of Rights—guarantee us freedom of worship, freedom of speech, freedom of the press, freedom against illegal search, and other rights that apply to all citizens. Regardless of how these documents read on paper, however, they would be meaningless without the court to administer impartial decisions and rulings. Therefore, the primary work of the court is to protect and keep alive all of the guaranteed liberties.

It is well for the law enforcement officer to remember that

the Constitution as written requires the courts to do more than generally safeguard these liberties. The rules governing law enforcement and legal process are, in fact, spelled out quite clearly in specific cases. One of the most applicable rules states that an officer may not enter a home without a search warrant issued by a court on "reasonable evidence." Also, no one can be held on suspicion of crime for an indefinite period without hearing in court the charge against him. And no one can be convicted of a crime which was not a crime at the time of commission. These and other concepts of liberty and civil rights will be discussed in detail later on. The point to be made here is that the courts are definitely an integral and essential part of the process of justice and law enforcement.

COURT SYSTEMS

Civil and Criminal Proceedings Compared. A "civil proceeding" is one in which the remedy sought from the court is money damages or an order from the court directing or restricting a specific course of action by the other party. It is to be distinguished from a "criminal proceeding," whereby the remedy sought is punishment of a party for some wrongdoing he is alleged to have committed. "A civil action is prosecuted by one party against another for the declaration, enforcement, or protection of a right, or the redress or prevention of a wrong." (California Code of Civil Procedure, sec. 30) "The proceeding by which a party charged with a public offense is accused and brought to trial and punishment is known as a criminal action." (California Penal Code, sec. 683)

The main distinction, however, between the two proceedings is that the civil action is brought by one party against another party (e.g., *John Smith v. Robert Andrews*) and the criminal action is brought by the people of the state against an individual (e.g., *People of the State of California v. John Smith*). The nomenclature of the parties involved in each proceeding is also different. In a civil proceeding the moving party is referred to as the "plaintiff." A plaintiff is defined in *Black's Law Dictionary*, third edition, as "a person who brings an action; the party who complains or sues in a personal action and is so named on the record." In a criminal proceeding the state, although it may be named as the plaintiff, may also be referred to as the "prosecution," i.e., the state is seeking to prove the guilt of the accused party. The responding party, i.e., the one being sued either by the plaintiff in a civil action or by the prosecution in a criminal action, is called the "defendant"—defined by *Black's Law Dictionary*, third edition, as "the person defending or denying; the party against whom relief or recovery is sought in an action or suit."

Degree of Proof. The proceedings themselves differ greatly in the degree of proof required for a judgment. In a criminal proceeding the prosecution must prove the defendant guilty beyond a reasonable doubt and to a moral certainty. In a civil proceeding the plaintiff, or moving party, must prove his case by a preponderance of the evidence. The jury in a criminal proceeding must reach a unanimous decision of all twelve jurors for a verdict of acquittal or conviction, whereas in a civil proceeding the votes of at least nine jurors are needed for a verdict.

The reason for the difference in the required degree of proof is that in criminal actions the presumption of the defendant's innocence is jealously guarded by the courts. One might say that the administration of justice is predicated upon the presumption of innocence. The requirement of all twelve jurors for a verdict is an example of how such a presumption is carried forth in the trial of the accused.

Code of Civil Procedure. The procedure followed in a civil action differs in many respects from that in a criminal matter. The reason is that in the civil action a party is merely seeking redress against another, whereas in the criminal action an accused person is standing before the court in a proceeding that will determine his guilt and prescribe punishment commensurate with the offense charged.

In civil proceedings there is no arraignment whereby the defendant is advised of the charge against him. An analogous procedure is the opportunity afforded a defendant to answer the civil charges by means of a pleading called an "answer." As in the arraignment, the answer will admit or deny the charges. The main distinction between the two procedures is that in an arraignment the defendant is physically present, while in an answer the reply is written and served upon the plaintiff. There are also time limitations within which to reply. A statutory time limit can be placed upon the defendant to reply, and in the event he does not reply accordingly the plaintiff's charges are taken as true and correct.

In civil actions, as in criminal actions, all of the procedures are statutory. The procedures are set forth in the code of civil procedure and must be strictly complied with or the party will forfeit whatever rights he has available to him. Each state has a code of civil procedure that sets forth the requirements that must be met for one party to bring an action against another.

With the myriad of different civil proceedings and types of civil actions, there is a great deal more procedure involved than in criminal actions. There are statutes of limitations in civil actions as well as in criminal actions, but so complex is our society that the number of statutes of limitations in civil actions far exceed those provided for criminal actions. The spectrum of civil proceedings affects everyone's daily lives, whereas the criminal provisions of our state affect a comparatively small minority. Although criminal proceedings take precedence on the court calendar, they occupy only a small percentage of the court's time in comparison with civil proceedings.

CRIMINAL PROCEEDINGS

Nature of Criminal Proceedings. The nature of a criminal proceeding is to enforce the law that ensures all citizens the right to life, liberty, and the pursuit of happiness and protection from violence and the criminal activity of other persons. It has the purpose of preventing crime through the judicial process and the allocation of punishment for those who disobey the rules and standard of conduct established for the functioning of an orderly society.

The criminal proceeding is also one that ensures against tyranny. It provides that all persons accused of a crime are entitled to due process. Even in light of overwhelming evidence at the onset of the accusation, an accused is entitled to a fair trial. It is an error of many a police officer to believe a man guilty because he has seen fit to arrest him and not to understand why the accused person should be entitled to a trial. Our system of justice is predicated upon the presumption that a man is innocent until proved guilty. If it were otherwise, the determination of guilt would rest entirely with the police officer. The police officer is trained to apprehend, *not* to decide guilt or innocence. This ultimate decision rests with the judge or jury.

TRIAL SYSTEMS

Court Trial. A "court trial" is one in which the decision of guilt or innocence in a criminal matter, or of the defendant's responsibility to the plaintiff in a civil action, rests entirely with the judge. The judge is the arbitrator of the facts presented at the trial. He has the responsibility to apply the laws of the state to the facts of the case before him. In a court trial the judge acts as both judge and jury. He renders a decision in a criminal trial as to whether the defendant is guilty or not guilty and, in a civil trial, whether or not the plaintiff prevails.

The procedure does not vary except that in the court trial there is no jury and any procedures necessary in the selection thereof and instructions thereto are eliminated (see Chapter 7).

Jury Trial. In a "jury trial" the decision as to the facts of a case are decided by the jury. The jury makes its decisions based upon the law of the case as read to them by the judge. The jury does not decide issues of law; that is the function of the judge. The jury only applies the law of the case to the facts presented to it during the trial.

THE AMERICAN JURY SYSTEM

The authority for the establishment of the jury system in the United States can be found in the Constitution, Article III, section 2, clause 3, which provides: "The trial of all crimes except in cases of impeachment shall be by jury."

Although the above provisions apply to federal law, the individual states have seen fit to include such provisions for jury trials in their constitutions. One of the basic reasons for the establishment of a jury system was the desire of the framers of the Constitution to remove the arbitrary authority from judges and establish a system of justice that was in the hands of the people. Without question the American jury system closely resembles that of the English courts, just as many of our laws are founded upon English jurisprudence. The jury system had functioned quite well in England, and the framers of the Constitution encouraged its adoption as a part of the United States Constitution.

KINDS OF JURIES

Juries have developed from the tribal custom of having several of the members of a tribe decide the facts of a dispute involving their fellow tribesmen to the present-day system of twelve jurors selected from the community. It should be noted that even in the most primitive types of juries one member of the tribe, usually the leader, was the presiding member and guided the jury in the laws of that tribe. The judge, in modern days, acts in this capacity. The jury only determines and decides matters of fact, leaving the decision as to the law in the hands of the judge.

Another type of jury is the "grand jury," which consists of members of the community selected by the judges. This jury does not decide ultimate facts, but functions as an investigative body of the community, recommending remedial action that it deems necessary to improve the community and facilitate the orderly functions of local government.

A third type of jury is the "coroner's jury." This jury is called to investigate the cause of a death. It does not function as a final arbiter of the cause of death but only recommends whether the defendant be charged with the commission of a crime. The decision whether or not to prosecute is then left to the district attorney.

GENERAL ASPECTS OF JURORS AND JURIES

One of the oft-quoted comments heard regarding the jury system is that jurors "do not listen to the facts and are swayed by the emotions of the case before them." The jury system, by its very nature, is subject to the emotions of the jurors. One must remember that the purpose of the jury is to determine whether or not the defendant, under this set of facts and under these particular circumstances, committed that crime. The jury must render a specific decision. It may very well be that the emotions in a particular case play an important role in the determination of a man's guilt or innocence. Laws were not made to be applicable to every conceivable set of circumstances. Participating and surrounding circumstances must be applied to each individual case.

A juror is an individual citizen selected to decide a set of facts in a controversy that has been presented in court, whether the controversy be civil or criminal. In a country as diverse as ours, it is seldom that many men will agree on every factual matter presented to them. All jurors have individual powers of perception and interpretation. It is the collective application of these powers in a fair and impartial manner that is solicited in a jury trial and that ensures the preservation of our system of jurisprudence.

SUMMARY

The American court system falls into two divisions, federal and state. The jurisdiction of each court depends upon the type of case, where the facts occurred, and the subject matter involved. The authority for the establishment of the federal court system is found in Article III, sections 1 and 2, of the United States Constitution.

The three primary purposes for the establishment of a court system are (1) to provide a means of due process for the citizen, (2) to provide an authority for the control of criminals, and (3) to protect our liberties.

Civil proceedings are distinguished from criminal proceedings in that the former action is usually an action between two citizens against each other, whereas the latter is one in which the state prosecutes a citizen for the violation of one of its laws. The degree of proof required in a civil matter is a preponderance of the evidence. In a criminal matter, the prosecution must prove the defendant guilty beyond a reasonable doubt and to a moral certainty.

QUESTIONS

1. What are the two divisions of the American court system?
2. What is meant by "exclusive jurisdiction"?
3. Why would the federal courts have exclusive jurisdiction in admiralty, patents, or bankruptcy matters?
4. Where is the specific legal authority found for the establishment of our court systems?
5. What article of the California Constitution refers to the California court system?
6. What are the terms for Supreme Court justices, District Court justices, and Superior Court judges?
7. What are the three basic reasons for having courts?

8. What is the main object of a judicial tribunal?
9. Is a civil action in which the United States is a party in state or federal jurisdiction?
10. Where may the procedural rules for the courts be found?
11. What is the distinction between civil and criminal proceedings?
12. Define a plaintiff; a defendant.
13. What is the degree of proof required in a criminal case? In a civil case?
14. Why is there a difference in the degree of proof required in the two types of cases?
15. Is there an arraignment in a civil proceeding? If not, what proceeding in civil court may be compared with the criminal arraignment?
16. What is the difference between a court trial and a jury trial?

3

court organization and administration

The organizational structure of our courts of law is not highly complicated. In fact, its simplicity is almost striking in view of the complexities of many other governmental agencies which carry a far lesser responsibility to the American people. The simple, straight lines of organization should not, however, be confused with the intricate machinery of judicial process. The peace officer's role in this machinery is one of daily acquaintance and frequent contact. If he is to fulfill this role in a professional manner, he must understand, communicate with, and adhere to the system. He is as much an officer of the court as judges and attorneys. This concept should be kept in mind as we look at the various levels of courts and judicial systems, and the peace officer should, at every level, identify his role in the overall picture.

THE FEDERAL COURT SYSTEM

Like most organizations that call for increasing responsibility and authority from the bottom to the top, the federal court system is

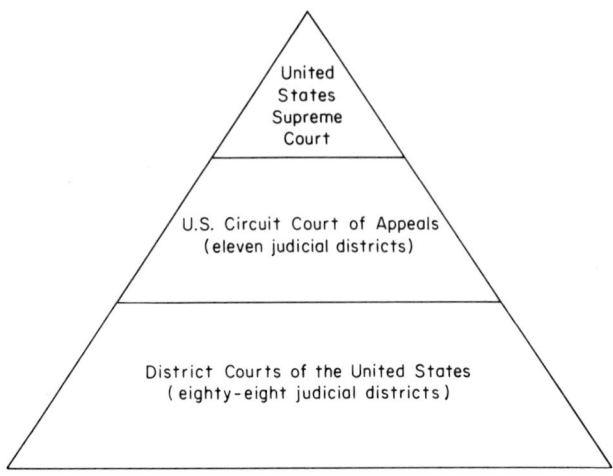

Figure 1 *Federal court system.*

built like a pyramid. The District Courts form the bottom of the pyramid and act as a base upon which the higher courts stand. The Courts of Appeals are the middle of the organizational structure and accept the responsibility of appellate jurisdiction from the lower level. The top of the pyramid is the United States Supreme Court.

The United States Supreme Court. The highest court in the country, the United States Supreme Court, was created by the Constitution in 1787. The authority for establishment of the federal courts is found in Article III, section 1 (see Chapter 2).

The United States Supreme Court has original jurisdiction over all matters concerning controversy to which the United States is a party. Original jurisdiction is also extended to controversies between two or more states, between a state and citizens of another state, and between citizens of different states, and to matters arising under the Constitution and laws of the United States and treaties made by the United States.

The Supreme Court also has appellate jurisdiction over cases remitted or remanded to the Court of Appeals or from the federal

District Courts. This simply means that cases other than those falling into the original-jurisdiction category may, when a question of federal law is involved, reach the Supreme Court by (1) appeal or (2) a special court order called "writ of certiorari" after having been tried in a lower federal court or in a state supreme court.

The President of the United States, with the advice and consent of the Senate, has the authority to appoint judges of the Supreme Court. Such appointments are for life. The Court is made up of nine judges, one of which is selected as the Chief Justice and presides over its sessions.

The Supreme Court has "discretionary jurisdiction," which means that it may decide which cases to hear and which cases not to hear. The test for an acceptance or denial of hearing is usually whether or not the case at hand is of broad and general interest to the national welfare. If this requirement is met, the Court will usually hear the parties.

The United States Circuit Court of Appeals. The second highest court in the federal system is the Court of Appeals. The United States is divided into eleven judicial districts, each of which has a Court of Appeals within it. In general, this court handles appeals from the federal District Court and reviews actions of the many administrative agencies.

The District Courts of the United States. The lowest federal courts are called District Courts and are found in each of eighty-eight districts within the United States. (Several more District Courts have been established in our overseas territories.) The District Court is the local federal court and exercises the majority of the cases within federal jurisdiction. In accordance with the United States Code Annotated, all offenses against the laws of the United States are tried at this level (18 U.S.C.A., sec. 3231); review and enforcement of administrative orders (5 U.S.C.A., sec. 1009) take place here as well.

The District Court also handles citizenship matters (28 U.S.C.A., sec. 1332), suits involving United States vessels (46 U.S.C.A., secs. 741-752), bankruptcy (28 U.S.C.A., sec. 1334), antitrust actions (15 U.S.C.A., secs. 1 and 2), copyrights (17 U.S.C.A., sec. 112), habeas corpus (28 U.S.C.A., sec. 2241-2255), and a multitude of other matters concerning federal laws and their application.

Separate Federal Courts. There are two other federal courts which should be mentioned even though they have little or no significance or attachment to law enforcement per se. They are (1) the Court of Claims (28 U.S.C.A., sec. 1491), which handles claims against the United States, i.e., for money damages, and (2) the Customs Courts (28 U.S.C.A., sec. 251), which have jurisdiction over matters relating to customs and duties.

JURISDICTION

Concurrent Federal and State Jurisdiction in Some Criminal Matters. In some instances a crime may be a violation of both the federal and state laws, e.g., *People v. South*, 122 Cal. App. 505 (1932). In this case the defendant, while in California, shot and killed a federal officer. He was indicted by the federal grand jury and was subsequently tried and found guilty. Between the time he was indicted and was found guilty, the local district attorney filed a complaint charging murder, a violation of California law. The court held that "the Court which first takes the subject matter into its control, whether this be person or property, must be permitted to exhaust its remedies to attain which it assumed control, before the other Court shall attempt to take it for its purpose," even though federal and state courts have concurrent jurisdiction.

In such an instance, the jurisdiction, either federal or state, that first takes custody of the accused has exclusive jurisdiction

court organization and administration 31

during the period of the trial. The question then is asked: Can the defendant be tried in the other court for the same offense? The defense of double jeopardy must be applied to see whether all of the elements for such a defense are available, i.e., was the defendant placed on trial for the same offense, on a valid complaint, before a competent court or with a competent jury? The one element that may be challenged is whether this is the same offense. Even though the law involved may be labeled a federal statute or state statute, the elements of the offense may be the same. If this is so, the defendant may have a defense of double jeopardy. It seems, however, that, as a practical matter, once the matter is tried in a state or federal court, the other court would not attempt to retry the defendant. Usually one or the other will proceed to trial, and this will terminate the prosecution.

THE STATE COURT SYSTEM

In the main we find that most states have divided their systems of courts into four distinct levels. Starting at the top we find the state supreme court, then an intermediate court of appeals, the lower courts of general jurisdiction, and the lowest courts, which are usually referred to as local courts of limited jurisdiction.

State Supreme Court. The primary function of the state supreme court is to hear appeals and review cases which were originally heard in the inferior courts. In some instances the supreme court also has other powers, such as the power to issue writs.

Intermediate Court of Appeals. The court at this level of the state system is usually confined in jurisdiction to hearing appeals from the inferior courts. In certain cases the decisions reached by this court will be final; in other cases the judgment may be appealed to the next higher court.

Local Courts of General Jurisdiction. At times criminal actions will originate in a local court of general jurisdiction. Whether they originate in this court or are originally heard in a court of limited jurisdiction depends largely on the seriousness of the crime committed. In some states the division of jurisdiction is determined by whether the crime is considered a misdemeanor or a felony. In civil cases, it is often the monetary value involved that determines jurisdiction. In almost every case the court holds the "power of review" over the courts of limited jurisdiction.

Local Courts of Limited Jurisdiction. The local courts of limited jurisdiction are so named because they are confined to cases that are generally considered to be minor in nature. Criminal actions are generally limited to misdemeanors and the preliminary examination of felonies. The most common names for these courts are justice courts (usually found in rural areas) and municipal courts (usually located in cities).

Municipal Courts. In urban areas of any size the volume of legal business can be extremely large. For this reason we often find that the municipal court will be divided into several branches or departments. These are referred to as traffic courts, small claims courts, and the like. Although each may have its own name and specialized function, they are all subdivisions of the system of municipal courts.

THE CALIFORNIA COURT SYSTEM

The authority for the system of California courts is found in article VI, section 1, of the California Constitution (see Chapter 2). The system follows the same general plan as most state systems. It is interesting to note and sufficient to say here that in cases of impeachment of state governmental officials, it is the state Senate that will hear the proceedings.

court organization and administration 33

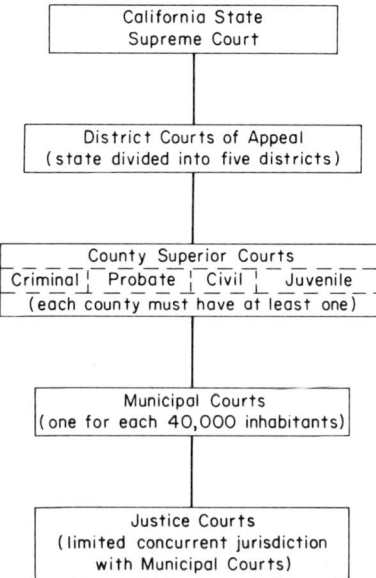

Figure 2 *California court system. A typical state court system providing for four levels of judicial process.*

The California State Supreme Court. The Supreme Court is the highest court in the state judicial system and is composed of one chief justice and six associate justices. The court may be convened at any time by the chief justice. The concurrence of four judges present at the time of the argument is necessary for a judgment. Whenever the chief justice is absent or unable to act, an acting chief justice shall be selected by the chief justice or the court (California Constitution, art. VI, sec. 2).

Most of the work performed by the Supreme Court consists of hearing cases appealed from the District Court of Appeal. It also has clearly defined appellate jurisdiction on appeal from (1) Superior Courts in questions of law alone, (2) Superior Courts when the judgment of death has been imposed, and (3) cases pending before a District Court of Appeal if ordered by itself to be heard.

Although the preceding constitutes the largest part of its

workload, the Supreme Court also has the power under article VI, section 10, of the California Constitution to issue certain writs, i.e., mandamus, certiorari, prohibition, and habeas corpus. The Legislature shall provide for the prompt publication of such opinions of the Supreme Court and District Courts of Appeal as the Supreme Court deems appropriate, and those opinions shall be available for publication by any person.

Decisions of the Supreme Court and District Courts of Appeal that determine causes shall be in writing with reasons stated (California Constitution, art. VI, sec. 14).

District Courts of Appeal. The Legislature shall divide the state into districts, each containing a Court of Appeal with one or more divisions. Each division consists of a presiding justice and two or more associate justices. It has the power of a court of appeal and shall conduct itself as a three-judge court. Concurrence of two judges present at the argument is necessary for a judgment.

An acting presiding justice shall perform all functions of the presiding justice when the latter is absent or unable to act. The presiding justice or, if he fails to do so, the chief justice shall select an associate justice of that division as acting presiding justice (California Constitution, art. VI, sec. 3).

By its very nature, the District Court of Appeal is concerned primarily with appeals from lower courts. The Supreme Court and the courts of appeal may affirm, reverse, or modify any judgment or order appealed from, and may direct the proper judgment or order to be entered, or direct a new trial or further proceedings to be had. In giving its decision, the court if a new trial be granted, shall pass upon and determine all the questions of law involved in the case, presented upon such appeal and necessary to the final determination of the case. Its judgment in appealed cases shall be remitted to the court from which the appeal was taken (California Code of Civil Procedure, sec. 43). The District Courts of Appeal, together with the Supreme Court and Superior Courts, also have original jurisdiction in proceedings for extraordinary relief in the nature of mandamus, certiorari, and prohibition (California Constitution, art. VI, sec. 10).

The Supreme Court may, before decision becomes final, transfer to itself a cause in a court of appeal. It may, before decision, transfer a cause from itself to a court of appeal or from one court of appeal or division to another. The court to which a cause is transferred has jurisdiction (California Constitution, art. VI, sec. 12).

It is interesting to note that case law also affects the administration of court business. For example, *People v. Walker*, 76 Cal. App. 192 (1926), establishes that a judgment by the District Court does not become final until sixty days after its announcement.

Superior Courts. The Superior Court is usually referred to as the "trial court" in that all principal matters regarding criminal felony cases and civil disputes are resolved in this court.

The Superior Court is created by article VI, section 4, of the California Constitution, which provides:

> In each county there is a Superior Court of one or more judges. The Legislature shall prescribe the number of judges and provide for the officers and employees of each Superior Court. If the governing body of each affected county concurs, the Legislature may provide that one or more judges serve more than one Superior Court.
>
> The county clerk is ex officio clerk of the Superior Court in his county.

The Superior Court is divided into separate departments at the option of the judges for the convenience and expedition of business. The usual departments include a Criminal Department, Probate Department, Civil Department, and Juvenile Court. It should be emphasized that the division into departments does not create a separate court. The Superior Court is a single entity even though it may consist of numerous departments.

Separate Nature of Departments. When, however, one department of a county's Superior Court is exercising the jurisdiction vested in that court, the other departments are as distinct from it as from other Superior Courts. Consequently, when a proceeding has been duly assigned by the presiding judge to one department for hearing and determination and the proceeding so assigned has not been fully disposed of therein or legally removed therefrom, it is beyond the jurisdictional authority of another department of the same court to interfere with the exercise of the power of the department in which the proceeding has been assigned. This does not mean, however, that after a cause has once been assigned it may not be reassigned or transferred, even irregularly, without jeopardizing the jurisdiction of the court. The power of the presiding judge is not exhausted by the original assignment of an action or proceeding. The jurisdiction over a cause, after it has been assigned by the presiding judge to one of the other judges for trial, remains in the same court, and the transfer of the cause from one department to another is not a transfer of the jurisdiction of the cause. Where a cause is thus reassigned or transferred, the situation is exactly the same in principle as though the judge of the department to which the transfer was made had been called into the department to which the cause was first assigned. The transfer does not vacate and set aside previous orders made by the department in which the original assignment was made, and those orders can neither be ignored nor overlooked in the department into which the cause falls by transfer.*

In that the United States Constitution, Amendment VI; the California Constitution, article I, section 13; and the California Penal Code, section 1050, provide for a speedy trial as a fundamental right of the accused, criminal matters take precedence in setting for trials and other hearings. Civil matters must therefore be set with deference to the criminal calendar.

Superior Court sessions are generally held at the county seat. The most notable exception is Los Angeles County, which until

---

* 13 *California Jurisprudence* 2d, 1954, sec. 195, pp. 754–755.

recently had the majority of its Superior Courts located in other towns within the county.

Municipal Courts. The practicing law enforcement officer will conduct business with the Municipal Court far more often than with any other because it is the Municipal Court's primary function to try criminal misdemeanor matters and to conduct preliminary examinations (see Chapter 8) for persons accused of a felony. In misdemeanor matters the court is limited to offenses which are committed within the county where the court is established (C.P.C., sec. 1462).

In addition to misdemeanors, "the Municipal Court shall have exclusive jurisdiction in all cases involving the violation of ordinances of cities and towns situated within the district in which such Court is established." (C.P.C., sec. 1462)

Unlike the Superior Court, the Municipal Court has limitations with regard to the monetary value and the type of civil matters which may be tried. The precedence of the criminal calendar over civil matters is, of course, well established in the Municipal Court as well as in the Superior Court.

Arraignments, i.e., sessions during which the accused is advised of his rights, etc., are generally conducted daily except Saturdays, Sundays, and holidays and at any time throughout the day. However, each Municipal Court usually has a set time for arraignments, most often in the morning hours (C.P.C., sec. 976).

A Municipal Court is established within a county judicial district, which is determined according to population. Each such district containing a population of more than 40,000 shall have a Municipal Court. Also, at least one judge must be elected to each district by that district's qualified voters.

Justice Courts. The Justice Court is very limited in its scope, especially as to the type of criminal case it may handle. Penal Code Section 1425 sets forth the jurisdiction:

Justice Courts shall have jurisdiction in all criminal cases amounting to misdemeanor only, punishable by fine not exceeding one thousand dollars ($1,000.00), or imprisonment not exceeding one year, or by both fine and imprisonment, where the offense charged was committed within the county in which the Court is established except those of which other courts are given exclusive jurisdiction and except cases arising under Section 272 of the Penal Code. Each Justice Court shall have exclusive jurisdiction in all cases involving the violation of ordinances of cities or towns situated within the district in which such Court is established.

Justice Court procedures for arraignment and other matters not otherwise provided for are the same as for the Municipal Court. It may be said that the Justice Court has limited concurrent jurisdiction with the Municipal Court (C.P.C., sec. 1462.1).

The Grand Jury.* A grand jury, as defined in Penal Code Sections 888 and 888.2, is "a body of the required number of persons returned from the citizens of a county before a court of competent jurisdiction, and sworn to inquire of public offenses committed or triable within the county." A grand jury contains 19 persons in counties of less than four million, and 23 in counties with four million or more.

Introduction. The institution of the grand jury is an ancient one, dating back to Magna Carta, signed in 1215. Its original and essential function was to protect the citizen against the tyranny or misconduct of his own government. As presently constituted it is chiefly an investigative body. It is charged with the duty of examining all departments of the county government, seeing that all accounts are properly audited, and, in general, assuring itself that county government is being conducted in the best interests of the people.

* The entire section on grand juries is adapted from the *Grand Jury Guide,* prepared and printed by the San Diego Grand Jury.

A grand jury is an entirely independent body, and no official has authority over it. The presiding judge of the Superior Court and the district attorney act as its advisers but cannot question its actions, provided they are legal. A grand jury can, however, question the actions of the judges and of the district attorney, as they are servants of the people and the grand jury represents the people.

Because of the confidential nature of a grand jury's work, much of it must be conducted in secret. Members of a grand jury are sworn to secrecy, which is an assurance to all who come to it with complaints that their matters will be handled in an entirely confidential manner. No one may be present during the sessions of a grand jury without invitation, and the minutes of its meetings may not be inspected by anyone.

Although they receive the most publicity, the conducting of criminal investigations and the returning of indictments are only one part of a grand jury's functions, at least in California. In some states all persons accused of felonies must be indicted by a grand jury before being tried. This is also true of the federal courts. In California the vast majority of criminal cases are presented to the court on an information issued by the district attorney. Action by a grand jury is sometimes requested when a case presents complications or when many persons are involved who may or may not be culpable. Witnesses can be summoned and questioned, and their testimony is given in secret. An indictment may then be returned, including named and unnamed persons.

In the case of a public official guilty of misconduct not necessarily of a criminal nature, a grand jury is the body best equipped to conduct an investigation. The official's associates and subordinates can be questioned in strict confidence and their testimony weighed. If it is shown that the official has been derelict in his duty, a grand jury may bring an accusation against him to remove him from office. If corruption has been demonstrated, he can be indicted.

Although a grand jury has the authority to initiate criminal investigations, experience has shown that the best results are obtained when matters are presented to it by the district attorney. Of course, if a grand jury has reason to believe that a district attorney is not pursuing a matter with sufficient vigor, it can spur him on to greater effort or proceed without him.

Unlike a trial jury, a grand jury does not pass upon the guilt or innocence of a person accused. It does not have to hear the testimony of the person against whom an indictment is sought, although it may do so. Its duty is to decide whether the evidence is such as to warrant charging a person with a triable offense. If so, an indictment is returned, to be acted upon by the courts.

Because a grand jury is composed of laymen, it can frequently view a matter more clearly than if its eyes were obscured by a mass of legal technicalities. From the court and from the district attorney it can obtain all the law applicable to a case, acquired in extralegal pursuits.

A grand jury is charged with a grave responsibility. The attention of the entire community is centered upon an active grand jury, and its every act is a matter of concern. The malefactors and the unfaithful public servants are uneasy, while honest citizens and the conscientious public servants are reassured. For this reason, the judges of the Superior Court endeavor to choose for the panels men and women of sound and mature judgment whose probity and civic interest have been demonstrated. Grand jury service is exacting and entails many sacrifices, but selection for it is one of the greatest honors a citizen can receive, one that offers him an opportunity to be of unequalled value to his community.

Secrecy of Proceedings. In addition to section 911 of the California Penal Code, which sets forth the oath to be taken by grand jurors, attention should be given to sections 924, 924.1, and 924.2, which read as follows:

> **Section 924.** Every grand juror who willfully discloses the fact of an information or indictment having been made for a felony, until the defendant has been arrested, is guilty of a misdemeanor.

Section 924.1. Every grand juror who, except when required by a court, willfully discloses any evidence adduced before the grand jury, or anything which he himself or any other member of the grand jury has said, or in what manner he or any other grand juror has voted on a matter before them, is guilty of a misdemeanor.

Section 924.2. Each grand juror shall keep secret whatever he himself or any other grand juror has said, or in what manner he or any other grand juror has voted on a matter before them. Any court may require a grand juror to disclose the testimony given before the grand jury by any person, upon a charge against such person for perjury in giving his testimony or upon trial therefor.

Immunity of Jurors. Penal Code section 924.5 has this to say:

A grand juror cannot be questioned for anything he may say or any vote he may give in the grand jury relative to a matter legally pending before the jury, except for a perjury of which he may have been guilty in making an accusation or giving testimony to his fellow-jurors.

A grand juror cannot be compelled to testify how he or any other member of the grand jury voted or spoke on any indictment, and a refusal to so testify is not a contempt [*Ex parte Sontag*, 64 Cal. 525 (1884)].

An indictment cannot be impeached during the course of the trial of the issues presented, thereby showing an alleged improper motive for its finding and presentment, and a grand juror may not be questioned for this purpose [*People v. Casanova*, 54 Cal. App. 439 (1921)].

Duties of the Grand Jury. California law empowers the grand jury to look into cases involving imprisoned persons, public prisons, or willful or corrupt misconduct of public officers, by the authority of section 919 of the California Penal Code, which states:

The grand jury shall inquire into:
(a) The case of every person imprisoned in the jail of the county on a criminal charge and not indicted.
(b) The condition and management of the public prisons within the county.
(c) The willful or corrupt misconduct in office of public officers of every description within the county.

One of the original reasons for a grand jury was to prevent any person from being held in prison indefinitely without having been charged with a criminal offense. We shall discuss this later in relation to other safeguards. For now it is sufficient to say that this is not a new development in law but rather was one of the first concepts to be introduced into what was to become a democratic form. It is curious, however, that we still seem to uncover misunderstandings as to the meaning of what appears to be a relatively clear and simple point of law.

Penal Code section 917 empowers the grand jury to inquire into the conduct of every public office: "If a member of a grand jury knows, or has reason to believe, that a public offense, triable within the county, has been committed, he must declare the same to his fellow-jurors, who must thereupon investigate it."

A grand juror, however, cannot force the grand jury to make an investigation of a particular matter or of a particular offense. It is the vote of the majority of the members of a grand jury that determines what matter shall come before that body [*Clinton v. Superior Court*, 23 Cal. App. 2d 342, 345 (1937)]. Penal Code section 917 stipulates: "The grand jury may inquire into all public offenses committed or triable within the county and present them to the court by indictment."

Examinations of Officials' Books, Records, and Accounts. In accordance with Penal Code section 925, the grand jury shall annually make a careful and complete examination of the records and accounts, especially those pertaining to revenue, of all the officers of the county, and report as to the facts it has found, with such recommendations as it may deem proper and fit.

If, in the judgment of the grand jury, the services of an expert are necessary for the purpose of section 925, the grand jury may employ one, at an agreed compensation to be first approved by the court. And if the grand jury further determines that such expert requires the services of assistants, it may employ them, also at a compensation to be agreed upon and approved by the court (C.P.C., sec. 926).

After investigating the books and accounts of the various officials of the county, as provided in the aforementioned Penal Code sections, the grand jury may order the district attorney of the county to institute suit to recover any money that, in the judgment of the grand jury, may from any cause be due the county. The order of the grand jury, certified by the foreman of the grand jury and filed with the county clerk of the county, shall be full authority for the district attorney to institute and maintain such suit (C.P.C., sec 932).

Needs for Increase or Decrease in Salaries. Every grand jury first impaneled in even-numbered years shall investigate and report upon the needs for increase or decrease in salaries of the county supervisors, the district attorney, and the auditor. Upon request, this grand jury shall grant personal interviews with the officials concerned. It shall have a copy of its report sent to each member of the Legislature representing the county in which it has been impaneled before the start of the regular session of the Legislature in odd-numbered years (C.P.C., sec. 927).

Needs of County Officers and Offices. Every grand jury shall investigate and report upon the needs of all county officers in the county, including the abolition or creation of offices and the equipment for, or the method or system of performing duties of, the several offices. It shall have a copy of such reports sent to each member of the board of supervisors of the county (C.P.C., sec. 928).

Lands Subject to Escheat. The grand jury shall investigate and inquire into all sales and transfers of land, and into the ownership of land, which, under the state laws, might or should escheat to the State of California. For this purpose the grand jury shall summon witnesses before it and examine them and the records. The grand jury shall direct that proper escheat proceedings be commenced when, in its opinion, the evidence justifies such proceedings (C.P.C., sec. 920).

Right to Hold Public Sessions. Whenever a grand jury determines that the subject matter of an investigation is one affecting the general public welfare and involving the alleged misconduct in office of public officials or public employees and decides that such investigation should be made in a hearing open to the public, it may conduct such a public hearing when directed to do so by an order of the Superior Court or the judge thereof. The conduct of the investigation and the examination of witnesses shall be the same as if the sessions of the grand jury had been held in private.

Public sessions of the grand jury are not encouraged, in the belief that they are rarely constructive. In most cases such a public hearing may have a prejudicial effect upon the subsequent hearing before a trial court of any person who might be indicted as the result of the public hearing. Full provisions and rules covering public sessions of the grand jury are outlined in section 939 of the California Penal Code.

Court Sessions. Location and time of court sessions are significant considerations for the police officer.

Location. It may seem very elementary that the location of the court should be known by the police officer. However, in large cities, or those in which a transition is occurring due to relocation of courts or court schedules, the actual physical location must be made known to the new police officer.

The officer, after being advised of the need to testify, should check with the district attorney's office to ascertain what courtroom the matter is being held in. In some cities criminal matters are handled exclusively within certain court departments, whereas in others it varies daily. The court clerk may also be consulted regarding locations of hearings and recent changes.

Time. The times for hearings are usually standardized within each community. The police officer should check with the court clerk and ascertain what time arraignments, preliminaries, and trials are usually scheduled. It is, of course, very important for a police officer to be on time for a court appearance. After an officer is with a department for some time, he will become accustomed to the court schedules. Prior to gaining such experience, the court clerk or district attorney should be consulted with regard to court schedules.

OFFICERS OF THE COURTS

Clerks. The clerk of the court is, generally speaking, the secretary to the judge and the person who supervises the work of the attachés of the court regarding the acceptance and filing of legal documents, both civil and criminal. He is responsible for the collection and proper accounting or filing of fees and fines.

Attorneys at Law. "An attorney is an advocate, counsel, or official agent employed in preparing, managing and trying cases in the courts." He is thus defined in *Black's Law Dictionary*, third edition. We may further say that as an officer of the court he is subject to the rules and authority of the court as applied to the practice of law.

As the definition states, the attorney is an agent for his client, and any of his acts within the scope of his employment may bind the client. For example, an attorney who appears in court for an arraignment in behalf of a client in a misdemeanor case is presumed to be acting in behalf of his client, and his representation as to setting the matter for trial is binding on the client.

The rules and regulations of practice for an attorney are governed by the State Bar Act, with related law found in section

6000 of the Business and Professions Code. The law also provides that the unlawful practice of law is a misdemeanor.

Attorneys, in addition to criminal prosecution, are also subject to disbarment or suspension as a disciplinary measure.

Bailiffs. A bailiff is a police officer, usually in the employ of the county, whose duties are almost entirely related to the court. He attends all sessions of the Superior or Municipal Court and generally supervises the security of prisoners and jurors. He calls court to order and keeps order in the courtroom.

Bailiffs also transport prisoners to and from the county jail and from the court, and, in some counties, they transport persons, adjudged to be mentally ill, to the state hospital.

Each department of the Municipal and Superior Courts has a bailiff. In smaller counties, which have Justice Courts, a deputy sheriff may be assigned merely for the trials and arraignments and then perform his regular duties upon the termination of court duties.

Judges. According to *Black's Law Dictionary*, third edition, a judge is "a public officer, appointed to provide and to administer the law in a Court of justice. [He is] the chief member of the Court, and [is] charged with the control of proceedings and the decisions of questions of law or discretion."

The qualifications of Superior Court judges are set forth in the California Constitution, article VI, section 15:

> A person is ineligible to be a judge of a court of record unless for 5 years immediately preceding selection to a municipal court or 10 years immediately preceding selection to other courts, he has been a member of the State Bar or served as a judge of a court of record in this State. A judge eligible for municipal court service may be assigned by the chairman of the Judicial Council to serve on any court.

If a vacancy for the Superior or Municipal Court exists prior to election time, the governor may appoint any attorney as judge for the remainder of the term. The qualifications of Justice Court judges are set forth in California Government Code section 71601:

> No person is eligible to the office of Judge of a Justice Court unless he either has been admitted to practice before the State Supreme Court or has within four years preceding his election or appointment passed a qualifying examination under regulations prescribed by the Judicial Council. So long as a person who qualifies for the office of Judge by passing such examination remains an incumbent of such office, he shall be eligible to election or re-election to such office. This section does not apply to the incumbent of a superseded Inferior Court who succeeds to the office of Judge of a Justice Court or is elected to such office at the first election of Judges pursuant to the Municipal Justice Court Act of 1949 or the provisions of law succeeding that act, or who seeks re-election to such office.

Magistrates. A magistrate is an officer having power to issue a warrant for the arrest of a person charged with a public offense. California Penal Code section 808 lists the following persons as magistrates:

1. The Justices of the Supreme Court;
2. The Justices of the District Courts of Appeal;
3. The Judges of the Superior Court;
4. The Judges of the Municipal Court;
5. The Judges of the Justice Courts.

THE JUDICIAL COUNCIL

The Judicial Council sets forth the rules of practice and procedure for the courts, as well as performing other statewide judiciary duties. The California Constitution, article VI, section 6, establishes the council in the following terms:

> To improve the administration of justice the council shall survey judicial business and make recommendations to the courts, make recommendations annually to the Governor and Legislature, adopt rules for court administration, practice and procedure, not inconsistent with statute, and perform other functions prescribed by statute.
>
> The chairman shall seek to expedite judicial business and to equalize the work of judges; he may provide for the assignment of any judge to another court but only with the judge's consent if the court is of lower jurisdiction. A retired judge who consents may be assigned to any court.
>
> Judges shall report to the chairman as he directs concerning the condition of judicial business in their courts. They shall cooperate with the council and hold court as assigned.

SUMMARY

The federal court system consists of the United States Supreme Court (the highest court in the land), the United States Circuit Court of Appeals, and the District Courts. The California court system consists of the California Supreme Court, the District Courts of Appeal, the Superior Courts, and Municipal and Justice Courts. The two Supreme Courts generally try cases that have been appealed by the lower courts. The two trial courts of the systems are the superior and Municipal Courts on the state level and the District Courts on the federal level. The subject matter handled by each of the courts in both systems is set forth in statute and case law.

The grand jury system's prime function is to protect the citizenry against misconduct in government. Its work is conducted in secrecy, and each grand juror is sworn under penalty of law to keep its affairs from becoming public. The grand jury does not pass upon the guilt or innocence of an accused. Its duty is to decide whether the evidence before it warrants an indictment for the offense. The grand jury is required to make an annual examination of the records and accounts of the offices of the county.

QUESTIONS

1. Which is the highest court in the federal judicial system?
2. Where is the authority for the establishment of the federal courts found?
3. In what cases does the Supreme Court have appellate jurisdiction?
4. Name the two ways a case can reach the Supreme Court.
5. What is meant by "discretionary jurisdiction"?
6. What is the number of judicial districts for the United States Circuit Court of Appeals?
7. What is meant by "concurrent federal and state jurisdiction"?
8. What is the name of the California appellate court?
9. Name three areas of appellate jurisdiction.
10. Do you see any correlation between the two court systems, federal and state?
11. What are the departments of the Supreme Court?
12. Which court does the police officer come in contact with most often?
13. What are the grand jury's responsibilities to the community?
14. Are the grand jury's sessions always secret? If not, in what instances are they not and why not?
15. Describe the functions of bailiff, attorney, court clerk, and judge.

4

accusatory pleadings and arraignments

THE PLEADING

An "accusatory pleading" is defined in California Penal Code section 691.4 as "an indictment, an information, an accusation, a complaint filed with a magistrate charging a public offense of which the Superior Court has original trial jurisdiction, and a complaint filed with an Inferior Court charging a public offense of which such Inferior Court has original trial jurisdiction." An indictment or information is used in Superior Court. A complaint is used in Municipal Court for felonies or misdemeanors.

The important factor concerning such a pleading is the factual background surrounding the filing of such a pleading. The usual sequence of events preceding the filing of an accusatory pleading is as follows. The police officer prepares a report of the facts which form the basis for establishment of a crime, i.e., the fact that a crime was committed, information concerning the suspect who committed the crime, the damage or injury which occurred as a result of the commission of the crime. Once the information relating to the crime has been documented sufficiently to incriminate the suspect, the report is then forwarded to the district attorney. After the report is reviewed by the district attorney's office, a formal accusatory pleading is prepared and filed with the magistrate. It should be emphasized that the district attorney has considerable discretion as to whether or not to file an accusatory pleading. In certain cases there may have been a crime committed but the evidence may be insufficient to implicate the suspect. An accusatory pleading is only issued when there is reasonable cause to believe the defendant committed the crime and evidence to support a conviction for the commission of the crime.

Information, Indictment, and Complaint. The basic distinctions between the three pleadings are that the "indictment" is the pleading used by the grand jury to charge a person with a crime; the "information" is the pleading used by the district attorney to charge a person with a crime; and the "complaint" is the pleading used by the district attorney for offenses triable in both Superior Court and Municipal Court. A complaint differs from an information basically in that an information is used exclusively for matters triable solely in the Superior Court and a complaint generally refers to crimes within the inferior courts' jurisdiction.

All accusatory pleadings, informations, indictments, and complaints are required by Penal Code sections 950 and 959 to contain the following information:

1. The title of the action, specifying the name of the court to which the same is presented, and the names of the parties
2. A statement of the public offense or offenses charged therein
3. The fact that it is filed in a court having authority to receive it, though the name of the court be not stated
4. The fact that if an indictment, it was found by a grand jury of the county in which the court was held, or if an information, it was subscribed and presented to the court by the district attorney of the county in which the court was held
5. The fact that if a complaint, it is made and subscribed to by

some natural person and sworn to before some officer entitled to administer oaths
6. The defendant's name or, if his name is unknown, the fact that he is described by a fictitious name, with a statement that his true name is to the grand jury, district attorney, or complainant, as the case may be, unknown
7. The fact that the offense charged therein is triable in the court in which it is filed, except in case of a complaint filed with a magistrate for the purposes of a preliminary examination
8. The fact that the offense was committed at some time prior to the filing of the accusatory pleading

Rules of Pleading. The rules of pleading for criminal matters are strictly controlled by statute. It should be strongly emphasized that unless the procedures set forth in the statutes are complied with, the charge may be dismissed in its entirety. For example, Penal Code section 72 provides that it shall be the duty of the district attorney of the county in which the offense is triable to file in Superior Court of the county within fifteen days after the commitment an information against the defendant. Therefore, if an information is not filed within the time limit provided by the statute, the charges *must be dismissed*.

The Penal Code (section 952) also sets forth the manner of charging the offense, i.e., the language which must be used to designate the commission of the crime:

> In charging an offense, each count shall contain, and shall be sufficient if it contains in substance, a statement that the accused has committed some public offense therein specified. Such statement may be made in ordinary and concise language without any technical averments or any allegations of matter not essential to be proved. It may be in the words of the enactment describing the offense or declaring the matter to be a public offense, or in any words sufficient to give the accused notice of the offense of which he is accused. In charging theft

it shall be sufficient to allege that the defendant unlawfully took the labor or property of another.

As a practical matter, however, the district attorney usually recites the wording of the Penal Code section which has been violated and uses forms that he has used time and again with the exception of the names and dates of the offenses. These forms have been tested previously for accuracy and have proved reliable.

The requirements of pleading are also applicable to prior offenses. Prior convictions must be pleaded and, of course, proved in order to secure the more severe penalty for the offense. The forms of pleading for such prior offenses are set forth as follows in section 969 of the Penal Code:

> In charging the fact of a previous conviction of felony, or of an attempt to commit an offense which, if perpetrated, would have been a felony, or of theft, it is sufficient to state, "that the defendant, before the commission of the offense charged herein, was in (giving the title of the Court in which the conviction was had) convicted of a felony (or attempt, etc., or of theft)." If more than one previous conviction is charged, the date of the judgment upon each conviction may be stated, and all known previous convictions, whether in this State or elsewhere, must be charged.

ARRAIGNMENTS

"Arraignment" means the bringing forth of a criminal defendant before the court to answer the criminal charge which has been filed against him. The purpose is to inform the defendant of the criminal charge and to permit him to advise the court of his response to the charge, i.e., whether he pleads guilty or not guilty.

The California Penal Code does not specify any particular time for the arraignment. However, it does provide that every public officer or other persons having arrested any person upon a criminal charge who *willfully delay* to take a person before a magistrate are guilty of a misdemeanor (C.P.C., sec. 145). The

accusatory pleadings and arraignments 55

only mention of a specific time limit is in Penal Code section 825, which provides that the defendant must, in all cases, be taken before the magistrate without unnecessary delay and, in any event, within two days after his arrest, excluding Sunday and holidays. This does not mean, however, that two days may not be an unnecessary delay. In some cases six hours may be an unnecessary delay depending on the circumstances. The Penal Code only sets forth a maximum amount of time, not a minimal amount, to bring the defendant before the magistrate.

Presence of Defendant. In misdemeanor cases, the defendant need only be present if he is not represented by an attorney. If he is represented, then his attorney may appear in his behalf. In felony cases, the defendant must be present under certain conditions set forth in Penal Code section 977. If the defendant or his attorney fails to appear at an arraignment, the court may issue a bench warrant for his (the defendant's) arrest, as well as order that any bail which may have been posted by the defendant be forfeited.

Procedure at Arraignment. In misdemeanor cases, the court or the clerk of the court reads the accusatory pleading to the defendant, unless the reading is waived by the defendant. The court then asks the defendant whether he pleads guilty or not guilty to the pleading. The court need not deliver a copy of the pleading unless requested by the defendant.

The defendant is also questioned as to whether the name whereby he is accused is his true name, and if he indicates it is not, an entry to this effect must be made in the court minutes.

Penal Code section 977 provides:

(a) In all cases in which the accused is charged with a misdemeanor only, he may appear by counsel only.
(b) In all cases in which a felony is charged, the accused must be present at the arraignment, at the time of plea, during the preliminary hearing, during those portions of the trial when evidence is taken before the trier of fact, and at the time of the imposition of sentence. The accused shall be

personally present at all other proceedings unless he shall, with leave of court, execute in open court, a written waiver of his right to be personally present, approved by his counsel, which waiver must then be filed with the court; provided, however, that the court may specifically direct that defendant be personally present at any particular proceeding or portion thereof. The waiver shall be substantially in the following form:

WAIVER OF DEFENDANT'S PERSONAL PRESENCE

The undersigned defendant, having been advised of his right to be present at all stages of the proceedings, including but not limited to presentation of and arguments on questions of law, and to be confronted by and cross-examine all witnesses, hereby waives the right to be present at the hearing of any motion or other proceeding in this cause, including when the case is set for trial, when a continuance is ordered, when a motion to set aside the indictment or information pursuant to the provisions of the Penal Code, Section 995 and following is heard, when a motion for reduction of bail or for a personal recognizance release is heard, when a motion to reduce sentence is heard, and when questions of law are presented to or considered by the court. The undersigned defendant hereby requests the court to proceed during every absence of his which the court may permit pursuant to this waiver, and hereby agrees that his interest will be deemed represented at all times by the presence of his attorney the same as if the defendant himself were personally present in court, and further agrees that notice to his attorney that his presence in court on a particular day at a particular time is required will be deemed notice to him of the requirement of his appearance at said time and place.

Dated:_____

_____
Defendant

_____
Address

Approved:
Dated:_____

_____
Attorney for Defendant.

Time to Plead. If the defendant requests time within which to plead, he is allowed a reasonable time within which to do so, as long as it is not less than one day in felony cases and not more than seven days in misdemeanor cases (C.P.C., sec. 990).

Pleas. There are six pleas which are allowed to the criminal defendant:

1. Guilty
2. Not guilty
3. Former judgment of conviction or acquittal
4. Once in jeopardy
5. Not guilty by reason of insanity
6. Nolo contendere

Guilty. If the defendant pleads guilty, it is an admission of every element of the crime. The defendant may be fined, sentenced, or given probation upon entry of his plea of guilty. In misdemeanor cases this plea may be made by the defendant's attorney. In felony cases it *must* be made personally by the defendant irrespective of whether he is represented by an attorney.

Not Guilty. A defendant who does not plead guilty may enter any one or more of the other pleas, including, of course, merely not guilty, which denies the commission of the crime.

Former Judgment of Conviction or Acquittal. This plea indicates that the defendant has already been tried for the same offense and been convicted thereof or acquitted. It is provided for in the United States Constitution, Fifth Amendment; the California Constitution, article I, section 13; and section 687 of the California Penal Code.

Once in Jeopardy. This plea is similar to the above except that it is not required that the defendant actually be convicted or acquitted of the charge—merely being placed in jeopardy is sufficient.

Not Guilty by Reason of Insanity. This plea indicates that the defendant did commit the crime but was insane when he committed it. Unless he pleads not guilty in conjunction with this plea, he admits the commission of the offense charged. If he merely enters this plea, there is only a trial on the defendant's sanity. It should be noted that when both pleas, not guilty and not guilty by reason of insanity, are pleaded, there are two trials (see Chapter 5).

Nolo Contendere. This plea means "I will not contest it." It was added to the California Penal Code, section 1016, in 1963. The effect of this plea on the defendant is the same as a plea of guilty, except that the former may not be used against the defendant in a civil case. For example, if the defendant pleads nolo contendere to a traffic citation for going through a stop sign, that fact cannot be used against the defendant in a subsequent civil suit brought by the driver of the other car. To collect damages as a result of the defendant's violation of the law, this plea can only be entered with the consent of the district attorney and the approval of the court.

Right to Counsel. According to California Penal Code section 987, "If the defendant appears for the arraignment without counsel, he must be informed by the court that it is his right to have counsel before being arraigned, and must be asked if he desires the aid of counsel. If he desires and is unable to employ counsel, the court must assign counsel to defend him." It is important to note that as a result of the 1963 United States Supreme Court decision in *Gideon v. Wainwright,* 372 U.S. 335, relating to rights of defendants in criminal matters to an attorney, the California Legislature, in 1965, added section 987a to the Penal Code. This code section is representative of the current legislation in the area of limited law and is therefore quoted in its entirety:

In any case in which *a person, including a person who is a minor, desires but is unable to employ counsel and in which* counsel is assigned in the superior court, *municipal court, or justice court to represent such a person in a criminal trial, proceeding or appeal,* such counsel, in a county or city and county in which there is no public defender, or in a case in which the court finds that because of conflict of interest or other reasons the public defender has properly refused to represent the person accused, shall receive a reasonable sum for compensation and for necessary expenses, the amount of which shall be determined by the court, to be paid out of the general fund of the county.

The board of supervisors may by contract provide that any public defender duly appointed or elected may charge reasonable fees to the Department of Corrections for representing inmates of prisons under its control, and the Department of Corrections may upon approval by the court pay such fees into the county treasury to be placed in the general fund of the county.

Counsel shall be appointed to represent, in the municipal or justice court, a person who desires but is unable to employ counsel, when it appears that such appointment is necessary to provide an adequate and effective defense for defendant.

STATUTE OF LIMITATIONS

Defined. A "statute of limitations" prescribes a time limitation within which to prosecute a defendant for a particular offense. In the event a person is not prosecuted within that time limit, he may never be prosecuted for committing that particular offense. The purpose of such a limitation is to encourage timely prosecution for criminal actions and to prevent procrastination on the part of the authorities to prosecute a defendant for an archaic criminal act. The general theme of criminal prosecutions is to provide the defendant with a speedy trial, and unless certain limitations are prescribed by law, there is a general tendency not to prosecute violators.

When it can be shown that the statute of limitations has expired on a particular offense, any prosecution, therefore, is completely void and without jurisdiction.

Specific Crimes. Certain crimes have no statute of limitations, that is, they can be prosecuted at any time after the commission of the crime. The specific crimes that have no statute of limitations are murder, embezzlement of public moneys, and falsification of public records.

All other felonies with one exception have a three-year statute of limitations. The one exception is the acceptance of a bribe by a public official or employee; its statute of limitations is six years. An indictment for any felony other than murder, the embezzlement of public money, or the falsification of public records must be found, and information filed, or case certified to the Superior Court, within three years after its commission. An indictment for the acceptance of a bribe by a public official or a public employee, a felony, must be found, and the information filed, or case certified to the Superior Court, within six years after its commission (C.P.C., sec. 800).

All misdemeanors have a one-year statute of limitations.

When Prosecution Barred. A criminal complaint, information, or indictment must be filed before the expiration of the prescribed time limitation, or the prosecution for said crime will be barred. The time period begins at the commission of the crime. The time is computed by excluding the first day and counting or including the last day. For example, "A" commits petty theft, a misdemeanor, on December 15, 1966. A criminal complaint must be filed no later than December 15, 1967. "B" commits burglary on March 15, 1966. The statute of limitations for a felony is three years from March 15, 1966. A criminal complaint must therefore be filed no later than March 15, 1969.

The policy of the law is so firm on the timely prosecution of crimes that if a complaint is not filed within the prescribed time periods, prosecution is forever barred. It is as if the defendant did not commit the crime in the eyes of the law.

accusatory pleadings and arraignments 61

It should be emphasized that filing a complaint and prosecuting a criminal action are not the same. Once the complaint is filed, therefore, the actual prosecution of the trial may be beyond the prescribed time. For example, if the complaint against "A" was filed before December 16, 1967, and the trial date was not until December 17, 1967, i.e., after the statute of limitations, there is no prohibition. As long as the action is filed within the prescribed time period, the actual trial may be beyond the time period.

Defendant Out of State. No part of the time that a defendant is out of the state may be used in the computation of time for the statute of limitations. Penal Code section 802 states: "If, when or after the offense is committed, the defendant is out of the State, an indictment may be found, a complaint or an information filed or a case certified to the superior court, in any case originally triable in the superior court, or a complaint may be filed, in any case originally triable in any other court, within the term limited by law; and no time during which the defendant is not within this State, is a part of any limitation of the time for commencing a criminal action." For example, "C" commits arson on April 1, 1963. He leaves the state for one year, from April 2, 1963, to April 2, 1964. An action may be filed against him no later than April 2, 1967.

Lesser Included Offenses. Some crimes can either be a felony or a misdemeanor, depending upon what punishment is imposed upon the defendant. If the crime is within this classification, it is considered a felony, and a three-year statute is imposed. That is, a felony-misdemeanor crime is considered a felony for all purposes until imposition of sentence. For example, "D" writes a bad check for $250 on May 1, 1965. Depending upon the sentence imposed, the offense may be either a felony or a misdemeanor. The time limitation within which to file a complaint is three years, or no later than May 2, 1968. Even though the judge may ultimately sentence "D" to six months in the county jail, which makes the crime a misdemeanor, the crime is considered a felony for procedural purposes.

SUMMARY

Accusatory pleadings consist of an indictment, an information, or a complaint filed with the court, charging a public offense. Indictments and informations are used in Municipal Court. The language used in an accusatory pleading must clearly designate the commission of the crime. It is usually framed in the language of the statute that has allegedly been violated.

The arraignment is the first time the defendant is brought before the court. The purpose of the arraignment is to inform the defendant of the criminal charge and advise him of his constitutional rights. The defendant may be represented by counsel at the arraignment and need not be present unless the offense is a felony. The defendant may enter a plea at that time or request the court for a reasonable time within which to plead. The six pleas available to the defendant are (1) guilty, (2) not guilty, (3) former judgment or acquittal, (4) once in jeopardy, (5) not guilty by reason of insanity, and (6) nolo contendere.

A statute of limitations prescribes the period of time within which a defendant must be prosecuted for a particular offense. Certain crimes, such as murder, have no statute of limitations. When the defendant is out of the state, the statute is tolled, i.e., the time period does not run.

QUESTIONS

1. What is an accusatory pleading?
2. What is the usual sequence of events in a criminal proceeding?
3. What are the distinguishing characteristics of an information, an indictment, and a complaint?

4. What information must be contained in an accusatory pleading?
5. In the event an information is not filed within the statutory period of time, what action must be taken by the court?
6. What facts must be stated on the face of a complaint?
7. Name the six pleas. Which of the six pleas may be combined with others?
8. Which plea can only be entered with the consent of the district attorney and the court?
9. What is the significance of the *Gideon v. Wainwright* decision?
10. Statutes of limitations may be "tolled" under what circumstances?
11. What crimes have no statute of limitations?
12. What is the statute of limitations for felonies? For misdemeanors?

5

post-plea and pretrial proceedings

SETTING THE CAUSE

All criminal matters to be heard within the State of California have precedence over civil matters. The importance of a speedy trial is covered in two Penal Code sections. Section 686 provides that the defendant is entitled to a "speedy trial," and the public policy of the state is amply stated in section 1050:

> The welfare of the people of the State of California requires that all proceedings in criminal cases shall be set for trial and heard and determined at the earliest possible time, and it shall be the duty of all courts and judicial officers and of all prosecuting attorneys to expedite such proceedings to the greatest degree that is consistent with the ends of justice. In accordance with this policy, criminal cases shall be given precedence over, and set for trial and heard without regard to the pendency of, any civil matters or proceedings. No continuance of a criminal trial shall be granted except upon affirmative proof in open court, upon reasonable notice, that the ends of justice require a continuance.

Automatic Dismissal. The public policy toward speedy trials is nowhere more fully explained than in the provisions of the Penal Code that state that if a criminal matter is not tried within a certain number of days from arraignment, the criminal charge is automatically dismissed. In misdemeanor cases the matter must be brought to trial within thirty days after arraignment, and in felony matters the defendant must be brought to trial within sixty days from the finding of the indictment or filing of the information (C.P.C., sec. 1382).

Waiver of Time. In the usual case the defendant, at the arraignment, is asked whether he wants a trial within the statutory period of time, and if he indicates he does not want a trial within such time period, the matter may be set for trial beyond the time limit.

INSANITY

The question of insanity becomes important in criminal procedures when the defendant enters his plea to the charges. When, as was pointed out in the preceding chapter, the defendant enters only a plea of "not guilty by reason of insanity," he admits to the commission of the crime. The only issue remaining, therefore, is whether or not he was insane at the time he is alleged to have committed the unlawful act. If the defendant is found sane, he must be convicted (C.P.C., sec. 1026).

Procedure Once Insanity Plea Is Entered. Upon the entering of such a plea, the court must select and appoint two or three psychiatrists, at least one of whom must be from the medical staff of one of the state hospitals. The psychiatrists selected are to examine the defendant and determine his sanity. They have the duty to testify whenever summoned in any proceeding in which the sanity of the defendant is a question. The defendant may also procure his own psychiatrist to testify as to his sanity.

Procedure When Insanity Plea and Not-guilty Plea Are Entered. In the event insanity is joined with other pleas, there is a trial on the question of the defendant's guilt, which is determined first. At this trial, the sanity of the defendant is conclusively presumed, i.e., he is presumed by the court to have been sane at the time he allegedly committed the act. Once he is found guilty, a second trial is held, generally with the same jury, at which time his sanity is in issue. If the defendant is found sane at the time of the second trial, he must be sentenced. In the event he is found insane, he must be committed to a mental institution unless he can show that he has regained his sanity (C.P.C., secs. 1026 and 1026a). The two separate trials are referred to as a "bifurcated trial." Although they are handled as separate trials, they are considered merely as steps within the same trial.

Burden of Proof. In an insanity trial the burden of proof is upon the defendant, i.e., he has the burden of proving that he was insane at the time he committed the act.

Test for Insanity. California follows the M'Naghten rule for the determination of criminal responsibility for committing a criminal act. The test in the M'Naghten case concerns whether the accused, at the time he committed the act, was laboring under such a defect of reason, from disease of mind, as not to know the nature and gravity of his act or whether, so knowing, he did not realize that what he was doing was wrong.

This test is sometimes referred to as the "right and wrong test," that is, it concerns whether the defendant knew the difference between right and wrong at the time he committed the act.

If he was unable to distinguish between right and wrong, then it is said he was insane. The right and wrong test is the majority viewpoint in the United States in determining the sanity of the accused.

Another legal theory that has won a certain amount of acceptance is the Durham rule, which holds: "The . . . rule is simply that an accused is not criminally responsible if his unlawful act was the product of mental disease or mental defect." [*Durham v. United States*, 94 U.S. Dist. Ct. App. 228, 214 F. 2d 862 (1954)]

One other view on insanity was established in *United States v. Currens*, 290 F.2d 751 (1960), in which the court stated: "The jury must be satisfied that at the time of committing the prohibited act the defendant, as a result of mental disease or defect, lacked substantial capacity to conform his conduct to the requirements of the law which he is alleged to have violated."

One can certainly see that in contrast to the use of a single right and wrong test the more modern rules on insanity relate in some way to the presence of mental disease or defect in the defendant.

PRESENT INSANITY

During the Trial. Insanity is at issue not only at the time the defendant commits a criminal act but also during the criminal proceedings. Penal Code section 1367 states that "a person cannot be tried, adjudged to punishment, or punished for a public offense while he is insane." The test for present insanity is whether the defendant understands the nature of the proceedings which are presently pending against him. In the event he does not, the court must order the question of his sanity to be determined by a trial by the court without a jury or by a jury trial if one is demanded by the defendant.

During the period of time a hearing is held on the defendant's sanity, all proceedings against him shall be suspended until a determination of sanity has been made (C.P.C., sec. 1368).

Before Execution. The defendant's sanity becomes important again after his trial and before he is executed. A man cannot be executed if he is insane. Once a defendant is delivered to the warden of the prison where he is to be executed, the warden, if he has good reason to believe that the defendant has become insane since his sentencing to death, *must* call such fact to the attention of the district attorney of the county in which the prison is located. The district attorney must then immediately file a petition in Superior Court asking an inquiry into the defendant's sanity, whereupon a sanity trial is held. The defendant, if found insane, is then committed to a state hospital until such time as he regains his sanity, whereupon he is returned to the state prison for execution.

CHANGE OF VENUE

"Venue" is the place, generally the county, where the alleged offense occurred, where the action is to be brought to trial, and from which the jurors will be impaneled.

The defendant may apply for a change in venue, i.e., to have his criminal action removed or transferred to another county, when he feels that he will not receive a fair and impartial trial in the county that has jurisdiction to try his case. The procedures vary from state to state. However, all states require an application by the defendant to the court and a showing by him that said trial cannot be heard fairly in that county.

In California, in the Superior Court, the application for removal must be made in open court and in writing, certified by an affidavit with a copy served upon the district attorney at least one day prior to the hearing on the application. The district attorney may file a counteraffidavit refuting the defendant's application (C.P.C., secs. 1033 and 1034).

Court's Discretion. It should be emphasized that the decision for a change of venue is solely within the discretion of the trial judge. His decision on these matters is almost always upheld on appeal.

Trial Publicity. We should point out that in light of recent Supreme Court decisions the discretion of the courts would appear to be much more limited. The case in point is the Dr. Sam Sheppard case in Ohio [*Sheppard v. Maxwell*, 384 U.S. 333, 16 L. Ed. 2d 600, 86 Sup. Ct. 1507 (1966)]. This case, it seems, will cause the courts to look with more caution to the publicity and feeling within the community toward a particular criminal action.

The Sheppard case involved the question of whether "massive, persuasive, and prejudicial publicity" had prevented a fair trial for the defendant. The Supreme Court decision was directed basically to the question of publicity *during* a trial. The trial courts were found to have mishandled the trial itself by not taking steps to limit or control the news releases and publicity. The Supreme Court reversed the lower courts and remanded the case for retrial. There was a refiling of the charges against the defendant and a subsequent motion for change of venue. This motion was made on the grounds that the publicity connected with the case precluded a fair and impartial trial in the county in which the murder occurred. The court changed the venue to another county. Therefore, in light of the Supreme Court's decision to reverse the case based on the amount of publicity and lack of control thereof as affecting the fairness of trial, the lower courts will now perhaps take more cognizance of pretrial publicity as a grounds for granting a change of venue.

CONTINUANCES

It was pointed out in Chapter 4 that the public policy of the State of California is to expedite criminal proceedings. The same Penal

Code section (1050) that emphasizes such policy also provides "no continuance of a criminal trial shall be granted except upon affirmative proof in open Court, upon reasonable notice, that the ends of justice require a continuance . . . No continuance shall be granted for any longer time than it is affirmatively proved the ends of justice require."

The generally accepted reasons for a continuance are as follows:

1. Physical disability of the defendant
2. Absence of a material witness
3. Absence of counsel for the defendant
4. Insufficient time to prepare a defense

The court has discretion to allow or disallow a continuance depending upon a showing of necessity for one of the above grounds by the defendant. As a practical matter, however, the district attorney will, in most cases, agree to a continuance if the attorney for the defendant makes a timely request, irrespective of the grounds listed above.

DISMISSALS

Misdemeanor Actions. A dismissal in misdemeanor cases is mandatory, unless good cause is shown to the contrary, when a defendant is not brought to trial within thirty days after he is arraigned, unless he has signed a written notice to appear, in which case within forty-five days after the latest date by which he has promised to appear, or the date upon which he does in fact appear, whichever may be later; or if there has been no arrest and he has not signed a notice to appear, within forty-five days after he has, by appearance in court pursuant to a parking citation or otherwise, submitted himself to the jurisdiction of the court; or if he has been released on bail or on his own recognizance, within forty-five days after such release.

Waiver by the Defendant. If the defendant requests or consents, either explicitly or implicitly, to a setting of a trial date beyond the periods set forth above, then no dismissal may be declared. The same is true if the defendant is brought to trial on the date so set for trial or within ten days thereafter. Nor can there be a dismissal if the case is not tried on the date set for trial because of the defendant's neglect or failure to appear, in which case he shall be deemed to have been arrested within the meaning of Penal Code section 1050 on the date of his subsequent arrest on a bench warrant or his submission to the court.

Defendant Not Represented by Counsel. In the event the defendant is not represented by counsel, he shall not be deemed to have consented to the date set for trial unless the court has explained to him all of his rights under Penal Code section 1382 and what is the effect of his consent.

Superior Court Actions. The Superior Court must order a dismissal unless good cause is shown to the contrary:

1. When a person has been held to answer for a public offense and an information is not filed against him within fifteen days thereafter
2. When a defendant is not brought to trial in a Superior Court within sixty days after the finding of the indictment or filing of the information or, in case the cause is to be tried again following a mistrial, an order granting a new trial from which an appeal is not taken, on an appeal from the Superior Court, within sixty days after such mistrial has been declared, after entry of the order granting the new trial or after the filing of the remittitur in the trial court; except that an action shall not be dismissed under Penal Code section 1050 if it is set for trial on a date beyond the sixty-day period at the request of the defendant or with his consent, express or implied, or because of his neglect or failure to appear and if the defendant is

brought to trial on the date so set for trial or within ten days thereafter.

Dismissal on Court's Own Motion or by the District Attorney. The court may, either of its own motion or upon the application of the prosecuting attorney, and in furtherance of justice, order an action to be dismissed. The reasons for the dismissal must be set forth in an order entered in the minutes. No dismissal shall be made for any cause which would be ground of demurrer to the accusatory pleading.

This type of dismissal is the one which is most commonly used by the district attorney when it becomes evident that he does not have sufficient evidence to proceed or that one of the essential elements needed to constitute the crime is lacking. Generally it is used when the defendant has agreed to plead to a lesser crime or to one of the counts against him in exchange for a dismissal of the more serious crime or of some of the other counts.

The court will, in almost every instance, grant the motion.

SUMMARY

The courts are required to conduct the trial in a criminal matter within a required period of time. The law favors a speedy trial, and unless the action is commenced within the statutory period of time, the charges are automatically dismissed against the defendant. A defendant who enters both an insanity plea and a not-guilty plea is entitled to two trials. The first trial is upon the defendant's guilt. If he is found guilty, he is entitled to a trial on his insanity plea.

Venue is the place of trial, i.e., where the offense took place. If the defendant believes he cannot receive a fair trial, he may apply for a change of venue. The discretion to change venue is with the judge. A great deal of pretrial publicity may result in a change of venue.

QUESTIONS

1. Why is a speedy trial important to the defendant? To the prosecution? To the court?
2. What is meant by an "automatic dismissal"?
3. Under what circumstances would a defendant waive time?
4. What must the court do when a defendant enters a plea of insanity?
5. When both a not-guilty and an insanity plea are entered, which trial is held first?
6. Who has the burden of proof in an insanity case? Why?
7. What is the "M'Naghten Rule"? The "Durham rule"?
8. What are the three times when insanity is in issue?
9. What is venue? When may it be changed?
10. What is the significance of the *Sheppard v. Maxwell* case?
11. When may a continuance be granted?

6

preliminary examinations

PURPOSE

A "preliminary examination" is a proceeding before a magistrate to determine whether a public offense has been committed and whether there is reasonable cause to believe the defendant committed the offense. A preliminary examination must be held before any information is filed in Superior Court. The examination, therefore, applies to felony matters whenever the proceeding is by information. In the event there is an indictment, there is no need for a preliminary examination. California Penal Code section 738 provides that "Before an information is filed there must be a preliminary examination of the case and an order (by the Magistrate) holding him to answer."

The preliminary examination also serves other purposes.

1. It preserves the testimony of witnesses who may not be present or able to testify at the trial. It is similar in nature to a deposition in a civil trial in that the testimony taken may be used at the trial to impeach the witness in his testimony.
2. It allows the defendant the opportunity to ascertain what evi-

dence the prosecution has against him. However, strategy of the prosecutor is often only to introduce sufficient evidence to hold the defendant over for trial, and he is not likely to produce all of his witnesses.
3. It allows the defendant to have the criminal matter disposed of without further proceeding when he can show that there was insufficient evidence to justify the criminal charge.

PLEA OF GUILTY

In the event the defendant pleads guilty at the time of arraignment, or at any time when the matter is pending before the magistrate, there is, of course, no need for a preliminary examination. In such a case the magistrate may fix a reasonable bail or, upon failure to deposit said bail, shall immediately commit the defendant to the sheriff. It should be emphasized that this being a felony matter, the defendant's attorney must be present at the time the guilty plea is entered. The Penal Code sets forth this procedure in section 859a and also provides that the guilty plea must be with the consent of the magistrate and the district attorney. It seems, however, that in practice a plea of guilty is very rarely not accepted. One exception is when the magistrate feels that the defendant is not mentally capable of making such a plea; then the matter will be referred for psychiatric evaluation.

WAIVER OF PRELIMINARY EXAMINATION

The defendant has the option to waive the examination. Upon such a waiver, the magistrate holds the defendant to answer, and then the district attorney must file an information within fifteen days in Superior Court. As a general rule it is unwise for the defendant to waive the preliminary examination in that it is an excellent opportunity for him to discover what evidence the district attorney intends to produce at the trial. Some defendants who are unable to make bail and are in custody may, as a matter of expediency, desire to make a waiver so that they can proceed to trial as quickly as possible.

THE EXAMINATION

Procedure: Time to Prepare. When the defendant pleads not guilty, the Magistrate must set a time for the examination and must allow not less than two days, excluding Sundays and holidays, for the district attorney and the defendant to prepare for the preliminary examination (C.P.C., sec. 859b).

Postponement. The examination must be completed at one session unless the magistrate, for good cause, postpones it. It cannot be postponed for more than two days at a time, with a maximum number of six days in all, unless consented to by the defendant (C.P.C., sec. 861).

Reading of Witnesses' Depositions. At the time of the examination the magistrate must read to the defendant the depositions of the witnesses examined on taking the information (C.P.C., sec. 864).

Presence of Defendant. The right to be confronted by the adverse witness is provided for at the preliminary examination. The defendant also has the right to cross-examine any witness who testifies at the hearing.

Again it should be emphasized that the district attorney will present only a prima facie case, i.e., sufficient evidence to show reasonable cause to believe the defendant committed the crime, therefore limiting himself to the bare essentials so that he will not disclose his total case to the defendant (C.P.C., sec. 865).

Examination of Defendant. The defendant has the right not to be examined. He may elect, however, to do so only upon being advised of his right to counsel (C.P.C., sec. 866). The question whether the defendant should testify at a preliminary examination is often debated. Many feel that the defendant should not do so because ordinarily the district attorney will have sufficient information or evidence to hold the defendant over and the defendant's testimony will merely give the district attorney a forewarning of the defense's case. In criminal matters the presumption of innocence is utilized to its utmost by the defense, and the defense attorney will not allow any inkling of his defense until the time of the actual trial.

It is therefore a very rare case in which the defendant will take the witness stand. One such instance is where the defendant feels his case is completely defensible from the standpoint of his alibi. Even so, he takes the chance that if he does not convince the magistrate of his innocence, his defense will be made known to the district attorney and his chance of acquittal at the trial will be minimized.

Examination of Witnesses. The defendant may produce witnesses in his behalf. The same provisions as those mentioned above apply to defense witnesses. Unless there is a very strong defense, it is usually unwise to produce a witness for the defendant because of the disclosure to the prosecution of the defense's case, and in the ordinary case the prosecution will indeed have sufficient evidence to hold the defendant over for trial in the Superior Court.

Exclusion and Separation of Witnesses. The magistrate may, during a preliminary examination, exclude all witnesses who have not testified. He may also keep the witnesses separated and prevent them from conversing with one another until they have testified (C.P.C., sec. 867). It is very rare, however, that the court will take affirmative steps to keep the witnesses from conversing, other than to admonish them not to do so.

Exclusion of the Public. The defendant has an absolute right to exclude the public from the preliminary examination. The only persons who cannot be excluded are the clerk of the court, the court reporter, the bailiff, the prosecutor, the attorney general, the district attorney of the county, the investigating officer, the officer having custody of the prisoner while the prisoner is testifying, the defendant and his attorney, and the officer having the defendant in custody (C.P.C., sec. 868).

The basic reason for the exclusion of the public stems from the very nature of the proceeding. It is an investigatory proceeding: one which is held to determine whether an offense has been committed and whether the defendant has committed the offense. It would be contrary to public policy to allow a public hearing in such a matter when its very purpose is to ascertain whether further criminal proceedings against the defendant are necessary. The examination may result in the matter's being dropped, in which case a public hearing would have an adverse affect upon the defendant for such a serious charge as a felony accusation.

It should be pointed out, however, that the occasions on which a defendant does in fact request that the public be excluded are rare. As a practical matter, the public does not usually make a practice of coming to court to hear preliminary examinations, and the only persons present are those mentioned as being allowed by the Penal Code.

There is also a provision that if the prosecuting witness is a female, she is entitled at all times to the attendance of a person of her own sex.

DISCHARGE

If, after the proofs are heard, it appears either that no public offense has been committed or that there is not sufficient cause to believe the defendant guilty of a public offense, the magistrate must order the defendant to be discharged, by an endorsement on the depositions and statement, signed by himself, to the following effect: "There being no sufficient cause to believe the within-named A. B. guilty of the offense within mentioned, I order him to be discharged." (C.P.C., sec. 871)

It is apparent from the above code section that the defendant is immediately discharged. It should be clearly understood, however, that merely because a defendant is discharged at this stage of the proceedings does not mean he cannot be charged again with the same crime. This proceeding does not amount to a trial to satisfy the requirements of former jeopardy (see Chapter 4), and therefore the district attorney may refile the criminal charges and this time be prepared to introduce more evidence in order to have the defendant held to answer. If, on the other hand, the district attorney has no other evidence to introduce, then, of course, the matter will not be brought forth again and the discharge will stand.

"SUFFICIENT CAUSE"

It is clear that the test as to whether to hold the defendant to answer concerns the existence of "sufficient cause" to believe he committed the offense. "Sufficient cause" is synonymous with "probable cause," which is defined by *Black's Law Dictionary*, third edition, as "an apparent state of facts found to exist upon reasonable inquiry, which would induce a reasonably intelligent and prudent man to believe, in a criminal case, that the accused person had committed the crime charged, or, in a civil case, that a cause of action existed."

In *Rogers v. Superior Court*, 46 Cal. App. 2d 291 (1955), the court said "sufficient cause" and "reasonable cause" mean "such a state of facts as would lead a man of ordinary caution or prudence to believe and conscientiously entertain a strong suspicion of the guilt of the accused."

HELD TO ANSWER

If, however, it appears from the examination that a public offense has been committed, and there is sufficient cause to believe the defendant guilty thereof, the magistrate must make or endorse on the complaint an order, signed by himself, to the following effect: "It appearing to me that the offense in the within complaint mentioned (or any offense, according to the fact, stating generally the nature thereof), has been committed, and that there is sufficient cause to believe the within-named A. B. guilty thereof, I order that he be held to answer to the same." (C.P.C., sec. 872)

In the event the offense is not bailable, the following words must be added to the endorsement: "and he is hereby committed to the Sheriff of the County of ——————". (C.P.C., sec. 873)

In the event the offense is bailable, then such fact must be added to the order (C.P.C., sec. 875).

COMMITMENT

If the magistrate orders the defendant to be committed, he must make out a commitment, signed by himself, with his name of office, and deliver it, with the defendant, to the officer to whom he is committed, or if that officer is not present, to a peace officer, who must deliver the defendant into the proper custody together with the commitment (C.P.C., sec. 876).

SUMMARY

The purpose of a preliminary examination is to determine whether or not there is reasonable cause to believe the defendant committed the offense. The preliminary examination also preserves the testimony of witnesses and allows the defendant to ascertain the evidence against him.

A preliminary examination is only held in felony cases and where the defendant requests the examination. The defendant has a right to be present but need not testify. Witnesses may be examined by the defendant. He may also exclude the public, the reason being that such a proceeding is investigatory in nature and does not determine the guilt or innocence of the defendant.

The judge may discharge the defendant if the prosecution has failed to present sufficient evidence to show probable cause the defendant committed the offense. Where there is "probable cause" the defendant is held to answer in Superior Court.

QUESTIONS

1. What is a preliminary examination? What is its purpose?
2. Under what circumstances is a preliminary examination not held?
3. Under what circumstances can a preliminary examination be waived?
4. What is the minimum time the defendant must be allowed to prepare for the preliminary examination?
5. The defendant has a right to be present at the preliminary examination. Should he testify? If not, why not?
6. Is the defendant allowed to produce witnesses at the preliminary examination?
7. Under what circumstances should the defendant not produce any witnesses?
8. Can the court exclude witnesses or the public from the preliminary examination?
9. If the defendant is discharged after the preliminary examination, can he be recharged with the offense?
10. Define and explain "sufficient cause."

7
the trial

In criminal proceedings, once the defendant has been charged with a particular offense, a trial must be held to determine his guilt or innocence. Of course, if he pleads guilty to the charge, the court will sentence him according to the punishment prescribed for having committed that particular crime.

A "trial" is a procedure or proceedings, held in open court, whereby a judge or a jury, after hearing evidence for or against an accused, renders a verdict of guilty or not guilty. The distinction between a court trial, i.e., trial by a judge, and a trial by jury is merely in the number of persons necessary to render a verdict. In a court trial the judge renders the verdict. In a jury trial the verdict is rendered by a unanimous vote of all twelve jurors.

ORDER OF TRIAL

In accordance with California Penal Code section 1093, the trial proceeds as follows:

1. The first order of business in a criminal jury trial is the impaneling and swearing in of the jury.
2. If a felony is being tried, the clerk reads the accusatory pleading and states the plea of the defendant.
3. The district attorney opens his case and presents evidence of the defendant's guilt.
4. The defense attorney presents his case, offering evidence of the defendant's innocence.
5. Each side offers rebuttal evidence.
6. The district attorney gives his first closing argument.
7. The defense attorney gives his closing argument.
8. The district attorney gives his final closing argument.
9. The judge then gives the jury its instructions.
10. The verdict is deliberated and rendered by the foreman of the jury.

QUALIFICATIONS OF JURORS

Section 198 of California Civil Procedure states:
A person is competent to act as juror if he be:

1. A citizen of the United States of the age of twenty-one years who shall have been a resident of the state and of the county or city and county for one year immediately before being selected and returned;
2. In possession of his natural faculties and of ordinary intelligence and not decrepit;
3. Possessed of sufficient knowledge of the English language.

Section 199 continues:

A person is not competent to act as a trial juror if any of the following apply:

(a) The person does not possess the qualifications prescribed by Section 198.

(b) The person has been convicted of malfeasance in office or any felony or other high crime.
(c) The person is serving as a grand juror in any court in this State.
(d) The person has been discharged as a trial juror by any court of record in this State within a year, as provided in Section 200.
(e) The person has been drawn as a grand juror in a court of this State and served as such within a year and been discharged.
(f) In a county with a population of not less than 300,000 as ascertained by the last preceding census taken under the authority of the Congress of the United States, or the Legislature of the State of California, the person, during the preceding two years, has actually served 20 days as a trial juror in the trial of cases in a court of record in this State; but a juror shall in any event complete his service as such juror in the trial of a case in which he may be actually engaged.

The clerk shall immediately remove from the jury list the name of any trial juror who becomes disqualified under this section.

SELECTION OF THE JURY

The trial judge has the duty to examine the prospective jurors to select a fair and impartial jury. Usually the judge asks a few questions as to whether or not any of the jurors know the defendant's attorney(s) or any of the witnesses to be called, whether or not there is any reason why the juror could not serve on this case, etc., and, more generally, whether or not they can be jurors. The judge then turns the matter of specific questions over to the attorneys, who go into greater detail regarding the competency of the juror.

The selection of a jury essentially follows this procedure:

1. The clerk of the court picks twelve names at random from the jury box.

2. The twelve jurors chosen take their places in the jury seats.
3. The judge asks the general questions relating to whether the jurors are competent to act.
4. The district attorney questions the juror in seat number 1 regarding the juror's feeling in a case such as the pending one.
5. The defense attorney questions the jurors.
6. After all jurors are questioned, the district attorney challenges either for cause or under his peremptory challenges.
7. The defense attorney exercises his challenges for cause or peremptory.
8. Once there are no more challenges to the jury, the jury is sworn and the trial begins.

TYPES OF CHALLENGES

There are two types of challenges for jurors, peremptory and for cause. A "peremptory challenge" is one for which no reason need be given other than that the person is not acceptable to the party exercising the challenge. A "challenge for cause" is one which requires some proof that the person possesses a particular disqualification to act as a juror.

Challenges for Cause. The challenges for cause are divided into two categories, general and particular. Penal Code section 1072 lists general causes of challenge as:

1. A conviction for felony;
2. A want of any of the qualifications prescribed by law to render a person a competent juror;
3. Unsoundness of mind, or such defect in the faculties of the mind or organs of the body as renders him incapable of performing the duties of a juror.

A general challenge will usually not be necessary at the trial level because the type of juror who would be subject to this type of challenge would ordinarily have been excluded from the jury list.

A particular challenge may be a challenge for implied bias, which, according to section 1074, may be based on:

1. Consanguinity or affinity within the fourth degree to the person alleged to be injured by the offense charged, or on whose complaint the prosecution was instituted, or to the defendant.
2. Standing in the relation of guardian and ward, attorney and client, master and servant, or landlord and tenant, or being a member of the family of the defendant, or of the person alleged to be injured by the offense charged, or on whose complaint the prosecution was instituted, or in his employment on wages.
3. Being a party adverse to the defendant in a civil action, or having complained against or been accused by him in a criminal prosecution.
4. Having served on the grand jury which found the indictment, or on a coroner's jury which inquired into the death of a person whose death is the subject of the indictment or information.
5. Having served on a trial jury which has tried another person for the offense charged.
6. Having been one of a jury formerly sworn to try the same charge, and whose verdict was set aside, or which was discharged without a verdict, after the case was submitted to it.
7. Having served as a juror in a civil action brought against the defendant for the act charged as an offense.
8. If the offense charged be punishable with death, the entertaining of such conscientious opinions as would preclude his finding the defendant guilty; in which case he must neither be permitted nor compelled to serve as a juror.

As a general rule, particular challenges for cause for implied bias are covered in the questions by the judge, but they may be asked by the attorneys in the event the court fails to inquire into those areas of implied bias.

The questions by the attorneys are almost always related to those facts which are covered as the "existence-of-a-state-of-mind"–type question. These questions can, of course, vary greatly, depending upon the type of case that is being tried. For example: "Would you be influenced in this matter merely because a criminal charge has been filed against the defendant?" or "Would you be influenced by what you have read or heard regarding this case?" or "Have you or have any members of your family been victims of a crime similar to the one with which the defendant is charged?"

In rather gruesome murder cases the questions may relate to the manner of death; for example: "Would you be prejudiced against the defendant merely because the victim of the crime was mutilated beyond recognition?"

In sex cases the questions might run as follows: "Would you be prejudiced against the defendant merely because he is the defendant in a child-molesting case or would you sit and listen to all of the evidence before reaching any conclusions as to his guilt or innocence?"

The above types of questions are very important in situations where the crime is of such a type that the mere possibility of its occurrence is enough to inflame the mind of the average person.

Questions to the jurors will also vary with the locale of the crime. For example, in a community where a well-known resident has been murdered, it would be appropriate to question the jury as to whether the mere fact that the defendant is a suspect in killing the victim would prejudice their minds. Where fish and game laws are enacted to protect a certain species of animal, any poacher who kills this type of animal will ordinarily incur the wrath of the local townspeople who may be called for jury duty. A standard question which generally covers this subject matter is "Would you be willing to have twelve jurors with your present frame of mind sit in judgment on your case if you were the defendant?"

Questions relating to prior service of the jurors in similar cases are also necessary to establish whether or not that factor will have an effect upon the juror's mind in this particular case.

In that there is a different burden of proof required for civil cases and criminal cases, the following questions are sometimes asked of the juror:
"Have you ever served as a juror on a civil case?" If the answer is yes, then,
"Are you aware that there is a different burden of proof required for a criminal conviction than a judgment in a civil case?" or "You are aware, are you not, that in a civil case all that is required is that nine jurors agree on a verdict whereas in a criminal case there must be a unanimous agreement on a verdict of either acquittal or conviction?"

It may safely be said that most defense attorneys will repeatedly emphasize the theory of law that "a man is innocent until proven guilty." Questions related to this point are interspersed with other questions relating to the precept that "a person's guilt must be shown beyond a reasonable doubt and to a moral certainty." The police officer who is experiencing his first jury case and watching the selection of the jury will probably be amazed as to how much this point will be stressed by the defense attorney, and in how many different ways. The purpose, of course, is to hammer the idea into the juror's mind that if the juror has any doubt as to the defendant's guilt, the defendant should be acquitted. The district attorney can, however, counter this argument somewhat by submitting an instruction to the judge indicating that doubt in and of itself is not sufficient for an acquittal. The following instruction, California Jury Instructions, Criminal, 21, is a good example:

> A defendant in a criminal action is presumed to be innocent until the contrary is proved, and in case of a reasonable doubt whether his guilt is satisfactorily shown, he is entitled to an acquittal, but the effect of this presumption is only to place upon the State the burden of proving him guilty beyond a reasonable doubt. Reasonable doubt is defined as follows: It is not a mere possible doubt; because everything relating to human affairs,

and depending on moral evidence, is open to some possible or imaginary doubt. It is that state of the case which, after the entire comparison and consideration of all the evidence, leaves the minds of the jurors in that condition that they cannot say they feel an abiding conviction, to a moral certainty, of the truth of the charge.

In summary, the questions on implied bias are as varied as the facts of each case. The questions generally will attempt to ascertain whether or not the juror has a state of mind or some prejudices that will in some way hamper his deliberations and not allow him to listen to all of the evidence before making up his mind as to the guilt or innocence of the defendant.

Judge's Decision as to Bias. The attorneys, of course, only ask the questions of the jurors in attempting to select a panel that can decide the case as objectively as possible. It is the duty of the judge to decide whether or not the answers by a juror reflect bias. If the answers to the questions indicate the juror cannot act with an open mind, then either the judge will automatically excuse the juror or the attorney asking the question will challenge the juror for cause. Once the challenge is exercised, it is up to the judge to excuse the juror or request further questioning which may disclose bias or prejudice in the case.

It is, of course, very important that the attorney be convinced that the answers given actually indicate such bias or prejudice before challenging the witness for cause. The reason is that if the judge does not feel that the answer by the juror so indicates bias or prejudice, he may not excuse the juror, in which case the only alternative is to exercise one of the allowable peremptory challenges.

It is better procedure for the attorneys to make either written or mental note of such borderline bias answers to questions and then excuse the witness on a peremptory challenge. This is because the judge may not allow the challenge for cause, in which case the juror may feel that the attorney does not like him and become prejudiced against the defendant. If there are no peremptory challenges left or if there is some other juror the attorney does not want and desires to exercise his peremptory challenge on that juror, he is going to be stuck with a juror who will feel some animosity toward him because the attorney saw fit to challenge him for cause.

Peremptory Challenge. As we have seen, a peremptory challenge is an objection to a juror for which no reason need be given by the attorney exercising the challenge.

Number of Challenges. Penal Code section 1070 states: "If the offense charged be punishable with death, or with imprisonment in the state prison for life, the defendant is entitled to twenty and the state to twenty peremptory challenges. On a trial for any other offense, the defendant is entitled to ten and the state to ten peremptory challenges."

In the event there are two or more defendants who are tried jointly for an offense, the state and the defendant each shall have the same number of challenges as prescribed by Penal Code section 1070, i.e., ten each or twenty each depending on whether the case is a capital offense. However, each of the defendants must exercise each challenge jointly. Each defendant is also entitled to five additional challenges which may be exercised separately. The state is also entitled to an equal additional amount of challenges as allowed to the defendants.

Exercise of Peremptory Challenges. The use of peremptory challenges is, of course, determined by the answers that are obtained to the questions asked by the attorneys. The attorney may feel that an answer indicates some bias toward the defendant but not enough to substantiate a challenge for cause. He therefore merely exercises one of his peremptory challenges and has the juror excused. Some attorneys will exercise these challenges merely on the basis of a "hunch," or the business the juror is in, or the way the juror looks. The reasons are many and varied.

Some prosecutors do not want male jurors on sex cases. Some do not feel that housewives are good on embezzlement cases. To a police officer it is sometimes bewildering that a particular juror has been excused. Suffice it to say that the attorney, whether prosecuting or defense, will have his reasons based upon his own past experience.

SWEARING IN OF THE JURY

Once the selection of the jury has been completed, i.e., when both the prosecution and the defense heve indicated to the judge that they are satisfied, the judge swears the jurors in.

In most cases the prosecution and defense will not utilize all of their peremptory challenges but will be satisfied with the selection of the jury before all challenges are exercised. In the event that the panel of jurors is exhausted, i.e., a complete selection is not made from those on the first panel, then the judge will summon a new list. In such case, of course, the jurors selected so far will remain. In the event there are no more available jurors on the jury list, the court is empowered to have the matter transferred to another county (C.P.C., sec. 1033.5). This, of course, will only happen in smaller counties, especially in a widely publicized trial.

Once the selection of the jury is complete, the judge will swear in the jury, i.e., advise them of their duties and responsibilities as jurors. After the swearing in, the trial actually begins.

TRIAL PROCEDURE

The Prosecutor's Role. The prosecutor or district attorney, as he is called in most states, is the attorney hired by the state or county whose job it is to prosecute offenders of public offenses. He is the person who initiates the proceedings in behalf of the people of the state against violators of state or local laws.

The prosecutor owes the duty to the people of the state to diligently prosecute a case once it has been commenced. Prior to the actual time of prosecution, which commences upon the filing of the complaint, the prosecutor has discretion as to whether or not to file a particular criminal action. However, once it has been commenced, he cannot cancel the proceedings.

The prosecutor's duty is to examine all elements of the case and make sure there is sufficient evidence before proceeding with a prosecution. If he feels there is inadequate evidence, he has the discretion not to proceed in a matter.

As was stated above, the prosecutor is usually the district attorney; however, the prosecutor may also be the county counsel, prosecuting a zoning restriction, or the city attorney, prosecuting a local ordinance. These types of offenses, though classified as misdemeanors by the local ordinances, are, in reality, semi- or quasi-criminal in nature. It is true that if the municipal code for a city classifies the keeping of barking dogs as a misdemeanor, it is in fact a crime. The courts and the persons who make up the jury do not usually regard such offenses in that light. It is usually very difficult for a prosecutor of one of these "crimes" to obtain a conviction. The usual ordinance of this type will also provide for a civil remedy of abatement, i.e., a proceeding other than criminal that asks the court to declare that the actions of the individual are a nuisance and therefore are to be stopped. This is actually a much more effective solution to the problem than branding a person a criminal.

The prosecutor or district attorney should be consulted by the police officer immediately upon his notification that the criminal matter is going to trial. In more serious cases, such as murder and felony manslaughter, the district attorney will be consulted immediately upon notification of the commission of the crime. This enables him to be in on the very early stages of the investigation and ensure that proper procedures have been followed by the police. In light of the recent Supreme Court decisions that direct the advisement of a defendant of his right to counsel, many large police departments have had an attorney attached to their staff. This attorney advises the police at the investigative stage and sees that their procedures comply with the court decisions.

With the less serious crimes, however, the prosecutor will not be present at the investigative stage, and it will be necessary for the prosecutor to review and discuss the facts of the case with the police officer prior to the trial. In larger cities, where the prosecutor has a large caseload, it becomes more difficult to meet with the police officer prior to the actual trial. Often the first time the officer gets to discuss the case with the prosecutor is a matter of minutes before the trial. It is strongly recommended that the police officer make every effort to see the prosecutor before the trial, even at the risk of making himself a nuisance.

The necessity of discussing a case with the prosecutor before the trial cannot be overemphasized. The defense attorney will have gone over his case repeatedly with the defendant, and it is likewise important that the prosecution's case be well prepared. Police officers sometimes feel that it is unethical to talk to the prosecutor about the pending case or about what they are going to testify to. The prosecutor will not tell the police officer what to say, but he will find out, for his own case, what may be damaging and thus be prepared to bring out those facts himself. This technique impresses a jury far more than allowing the defense to raise the damaging points. It then appears that the prosecutor has been hiding something.

Often the defense attorney will ask the police officer on the stand whether or not he has discussed the matter with the prosecutor prior to his testifying. The police officers should answer yes if such is the case. It is no secret that the police officer discusses the case with the prosecution, and if the answer is truthful, the matter will be dropped by the defense attorney.

Full cooperation should always be the keynote of relations between the police department and the prosecutor's office. Both parties are charged with a public duty to prosecute the offender of state and local laws. The prosecutor may, in some instances, not handle the matter the way the police feel it should be handled. This, however, is not within the police officer's purview. The prosecutor may have reasons for not offering certain items of evidence. His discretion should not be interfered with. This, however, does not preclude the police officer from making suggestions or reminding the prosecutor if he has forgotten an item. A close rapport must be maintained between the two entities for the successful enforcement and prosecution of criminal matters.

The Defense Counsel's Role. Article I, section 13, of the California Constitution states: "In criminal prosecutions in any court, whatever, the party accused shall have the right . . . to appear and defend, in person and with counsel."

The defense attorney's job is to protect the defendant's rights and ensure that the processes of justice are afforded his client. He is the person who accounts for the checks and balances system of justice. He must see that the defendant receives a fair trial. The question most often asked of defense lawyers by police officers is "How can you defend a person who you may think is guilty?" The answer is simple. The law presumes every person accused of a crime innocent until proved guilty beyond a reasonable doubt and to a moral certainty. It is, therefore, presumptuous for a defense attorney to make a judgment.

Of course, there may be instances when the circumstantial evidence overwhelmingly points to the guilt of the accused. It is still incumbent upon the defense attorney to ensure that all of the defendant's rights have been protected, i.e., that the arrest was proper, the evidence obtained was admissible, and the procedural steps necessary to afford all persons their constitutional rights have been accomplished.

If it were not for such a system of justice, a decision as to a person's guilt could be made arbitrarily and a police state, such as exists in certain foreign countries, would be the result. Too often the arresting party forgets that not all the persons he arrests are guilty of the crime charged, and in the event circumstances were such that he was accused of a crime that he did not commit, he would want the full protection afforded by law.

It is true that many of those who avail themselves of the procedural defenses and cloak of protection afforded by the constitutional rights are the criminal element. One must remember that the laws are set forth for the public at large and it is not inconceivable that the defendant may be unjustly accused. It is for this reason that the presumption of innocence must be preserved if the administration of justice is to function for the protection of all persons.

The duty of a defense attorney as well as a prosecutor is set forth in the American Bar Association Canon number 5:

> It is the right of the lawyer to undertake the defense of a person accused of crime, regardless of his personal opinion as to the guilt of the accused; otherwise innocent persons, victims only of suspicious circumstances, might be denied proper defense. Having undertaken such defense, the lawyer is bound, by all fair and honorable means, to present every defense that the law of the land permits, to the end that no person may be deprived of life or liberty, but by due process of law.
>
> The primary duty of a lawyer engaged in public prosecution is not to convict, but to see that justice is done. The suppression of facts or the secreting of witnesses capable of establishing the innocence of the accused is highly reprehensible.

Once consulted by the defendant, the defense attorney must endeavor to obtain all of the facts surrounding the crime with which the defendant is charged. Unless the defense attorney does so, he is in no position to prepare a defense. A thorough discussion with his client will reveal a basic foundation for a defense. It may become necessary to interview others who may have been witnesses to the alleged criminal act. It is not uncommon for defense attorneys to spend a great deal of time and effort conducting an investigation.

A large defense firm may hire a private investigator to interview witnesses or collect facts. The only deficiency in this technique is that a written statement may seem completely different when spoken by the witness. The witness's demeanor is very *the trial*

important to a defense. Often a witness will make such a poor impression that whatever he says will be misinterpreted. The defense attorney will usually interview the witness before the trial and make a decision as to whether his testimony will be of any assistance to the defense.

The defense also has the power to subpoena witnesses for the trial. The defense attorney should not depend upon the prosecuting attorney to produce all witnesses because the latter may have decided not to use a witness whose testimony could prove favorable to the defense.

There is no substitute for being well prepared for the trial. An attorney, whether prosecuting or defense, who prepares his case will always fare better than the unprepared. It may appear to the observer that the attorneys merely walk into court and play it by ear. This is not the case, and the police officer can be of tremendous assistance by having his case prepared as a preliminary step in the administration of justice.

The Public Defender. The public defender is an attorney paid by the county to defend indigent persons accused of crimes. Until recently, attorneys were appointed by the courts to defend persons accused of the more serious crimes. It was not the general practice of the courts to appoint an attorney to defend a person for misdemeanors. A Supreme Court case alluded to earlier, *Gideon v. Wainwright,* 372 U.S. 335 (1963), set forth the basic premise that all persons are entitled to an attorney no matter what the classification of the crime. The court said in the Gideon case:

> The fact is that in deciding as it did—that "appointment of counsel is not a fundamental right, essential to a fair trial"— the Court in *Betts v. Brady* made an abrupt break with its own well-considered precedents. In returning to these old precedents, sounder we believe than the new, we but restore constitutional principles established to achieve a fair system of justice. Not only these precedents but also reason and reflection require us to recognize that in our adversary system of criminal jus-

tice, any person haled into court, who is too poor to hire a lawyer, cannot be assured a fair trial unless counsel is provided for him. This seems to us to be an obvious truth. Governments, both state and federal, quite properly spend vast sums of money to establish machinery to try defendants accused of crime. Lawyers to prosecute are everywhere deemed essential to protect the public's interest in an orderly society. Similarly, there are few defendants charged with crime, few indeed, who fail to hire the best lawyers they can get to prepare and present their defenses. That government hires lawyers to prosecute and defendants who have the money hire lawyers to defend are the strongest indications of the widespread belief that lawyers in criminal courts are necessities, not luxuries. The right of one charged with crime to counsel may not be deemed fundamental and essential to fair trials in some countries, but it is in ours.

Since the Gideon case, most counties in California have provided for a public defender. Section 27700 of the California Government Code states: "The board of supervisors of any county may establish the office of public defender for the county. Any county may join with one or more counties to establish and maintain the office of public defender to serve such counties."

Section 27705 of the Government Code provides that "In counties of the first, second and third classes, the public defender shall devote all his time to the duties of his office and shall not engage in the practice of law except in the capacity of public defender."

Section 22706a provides:

> The public defender shall perform the following duties: Upon request of the defendant or upon order of the court, he shall defend, without expense to the defendant, any person who is not financially able to employ counsel and who is charged with the commission of any contempt or offense triable in the superior, *municipal or justice courts* at all stages of the proceedings, including the preliminary examination. The public defender shall, upon request, give counsel and advice to such person about any charge against him upon which the public defender

is conducting the defense, and shall prosecute all appeals to a higher court or courts of any person who has been convicted, where, in his opinion, the appeal will or might reasonably be expected to result in the reversal or modification of the judgment of conviction.

In larger counties the public defender's office is as large as the district attorney's office, and the counties appropriate funds to provide them with investigators. These recent developments clearly show the courts' growing concern for the protection of the accused, and the public defender's system is but one more example of this movement.

It should be noted in passing that the police departments are also approaching this area with more vigor. As was mentioned earlier, certain police departments now have full-time attorneys available on call to answer questions from the field pertaining to proper arrest procedure.

Opening Statement. An opening statement is made by the prosecution to advise the jury of what the prosecution intends to prove in its case. This is a general outline designed to assist and guide the jury or the court. The length of the statement will vary with the type of crime. If the crime is very serious or the facts are complex, the statement will be longer. Generally speaking, opening statements by the prosecution are brief and to the point.

The defense is also entitled to an opening statement. However, it is not made until the prosecution's case has been presented. Prior to the defense's presentation of evidence, it too will make a statement that will give the jury a general outline of the elements of its case.

Objections. When evidence is offered that is not admissible because of its immateriality, irrelevancy, or incompetency, an objection will be made to the court. It must be remembered that in a jury trial the judge rules upon all evidence. In the event an objection is made by either the prosecution or the defense, the judge will decide whether or not to sustain or overrule the objection.

Timely. An objection must be timely, i.e., it must be made as soon as it becomes apparent to the attorney that the evidence is inadmissible. It should be made before the witness has an opportunity to answer the questions. The failure to object will act as a waiver of an exclusion of the evidence.

Types of Objections. An objection may be based upon different theories. The form of the question may be immaterial, i.e., not connected with the issue before the court. It may be inflammatory. It may be prejudicial.

The attorney making the objection must be specific as to his objection unless, of course, the question he is objecting to is flagrantly objectionable or inadmissible; then the court will sustain the objection without any need for the reasoning behind the objection.

Need for Objections. Constant objections by either attorney may have an adverse effect upon the jury. Juries may get the impression that the defense attorney is trying to hide something, and his constant objections will only call the attention of the jury to the very point he is trying to avoid.

In many instances, it is better tactics not to constantly object. This does not mean that the attorneys should allow all inadmissible evidence to be allowed. The primary consideration in an objection is to make the jury understand that it is based upon sound reasoning and has the aim of promoting justice and fairness.

Presentation of Evidence. The usual procedure for the presentation of evidence at a criminal trial is for the prosecutor to initiate the proceeding. The prosecutor will call his witnesses, who will be examined by himself. This is called "direct examination." The witness will testify to certain facts as elicited by the questions of the prosecutor. Once the witness has testified on direct examination, he will be questioned by the defense. This questioning is called "cross-examination." The rules of direct and cross-examination differ. On direct examination, no leading questions may be asked. A "leading question" is one that suggests the answer to the witness; e.g., "You were in the deceased's home the evening of December 21, 1966, were you not?" On cross-examination, leading questions are allowed. The reason is that the purpose of cross-examination is to get at the truth, and greater leeway is allowed on the questioning of the witness. After cross-examination the witness may again be examined by the prosecution on re-direct, and after re-direct the witness may be examined on re-cross-examination.

Evidence will be introduced with each of the witnesses questioned by the prosecution. The evidence presented will be in the form of oral testimony or the identification of certain physical exhibits. Once the item, for example, a gun, is identified by the witness, the prosecuting attorney will offer it as evidence in his case. If the defense attorney has any objections, he must present them at the time the evidence is offered or else he waives his right to have the evidence excluded. If an objection is made to the evidence, the court must rule on its admissibility.

The prosecution may call as many witnesses and introduce as many exhibits as the court will allow. Generally speaking, the courts will not in any way limit the number of exhibits and witnesses. In a relatively simple offense, however, the court may suggest that witnesses are merely cumulative and will not add anything to the case which has already been presented.

Once the prosecution has presented its evidence and rested its case, the defense offers its evidence. The procedure is the same as set forth above, except, of course, the evidence will tend to diminish that presented by the prosecution or will offer a defense for having committed the alleged offense.

Upon the resting of the defense, the prosecution may offer evidence in rebuttal. Rebuttal evidence is that which tends to refute the defense's case. Rebuttal evidence is, of course, subject to cross-examination. The defense is also entitled to offer evidence in rejoinder, that is, evidence which refutes the rebuttal evidence.

In summary, the basic stages of the presentation of evidence are as follows:

I. The prosecution opens its case and presents its evidence.
   A. The witness is questioned by the prosecution on direct examination.
   B. The witness is questioned by the defense on cross-examination.
      1. The prosecution may ask more questions on re-direct.
      2. The defense may ask more questions on re-cross-examination.
II. The prosecution, after presenting its evidence, rests its case.
III. The defense opens its case and presents its evidence that tends to refute the prosecution's evidence.
   A. The witness is questioned by the defense on direct examination.
   B. The witness is questioned by the prosecution on cross-examination.
      1. The defense may ask more questions in re-direct.
      2. The prosecution may ask more questions on re-cross-examination.
IV. The defense, after presenting its evidence, rests its case.
V. The prosecution may offer evidence in rebuttal. The same procedures as to direct and cross-examination apply.
VI. The defendant may offer evidence in rejoinder. The same procedures as to direct and cross-examination apply.

Once the case has been submitted, it is time for each side to present its final argument and submit the case to the jury.

Final Argument. The prosecution and the defense have a statutory right to a final argument. Section 1093.5 of the Penal Code provides:

When the evidence is concluded, unless the case is submitted on either side, or on both sides, without argument, the district attorney, or other counsel for the people, and counsel for the defendant, may argue the case to the court and jury; the district attorney, or other counsel for the people, opening the argument and having the right to close.

In a "capital case," i.e., one in which the punishment is death, two counsel on each side are entitled to argue the case. In other cases the court has the discretion to restrict the argument to one attorney on each side (C.P.C., sec. 1095).

Procedure. The procedure for final argument is as follows:

1. The prosecuting attorney argues his case. His argument is referred to as the "opening argument."
2. The defense attorney argues his case.
3. The prosecuting attorney presents his closing argument.

It can be seen, therefore, that the prosecution has two final arguments to the defense's one.

Contents of a Final Argument. The prosecuting attorney will ordinarily confine his argument to the failure on the part of the defense to offer sufficient proof of the innocence of the defendant. His remarks will revolve around the evidence which has been received by the court and how said evidence incriminates the defendant.

The defense attorney is allowed a greater latitude within which to argue. His argument, however, will generally be directly related to the failure on the part of the prosecution to overcome the presumption of innocence and prove the defendant's guilt to a moral certainty. Generally speaking, however, his argument may range to any matter which is related to the case. He may not, of course, argue to any facts which are outside of the court record. Nor may he argue on matters of law or make misstatements pertaining to the law.

Instructions to the Jury. Once the cause has been argued by the prosecution and defense, the judge instructs the jury on the law. Section 1093.6 of the Penal Code provides that "the judge may then charge [instruct] the jury, and must do so on any points of law pertinent to the issue. . . ."

Instructions to the jury are no more than an explanation of what law is applicable to the case being tried. In an assault case the instruction will set forth the requirements and elements of the crime. It will charge the jury that those elements must be present before a verdict of guilty can be rendered.

Procedure and Content. Counsel for the prosecution and for the defense submit instructions to the judge in writing before commencement of the final argument. Penal Code section 1093.5 provides:

> In any criminal case which is being tried before the court with a jury, all requests for instructions on points of law must be made to the court and all proposed instructions must be delivered to the court before commencement of argument. Before the commencement of the argument, the court, on request of counsel, must: (1) decide whether to give, refuse, or modify the proposed instructions; (2) decide which instructions shall be given in addition to those proposed, if any; and (3) advise counsel of all instructions to be given. However, if during the argument, issues are raised which have not been covered by instructions given or refused, the court may, on request of counsel, give additional instructions on the subject matter thereof.

The instructions are then read by the judge, and he may read the whole instruction, modifying it or rejecting it. His rejection is limited in the case for the defendant. It is error not to instruct on fundamental provisions. The instructions themselves may be quotations from a code section, such as "Assault is defined as an unlawful attempt, coupled with a present ability, to commit a violent injury on the person of another." (C.P.C., sec. 240) Or, the Penal Code section dealing with the presumption of innocence will be quoted in its entirety:

> A defendant in a criminal action is presumed to be innocent until the contrary is proved, and in case of a reasonable doubt whether his guilt is satisfactorily shown, he is entitled to an acquittal, but the effect of this presumption is only to place upon the state the burden of proving him guilty beyond a reasonable doubt. Reasonable doubt is defined as follows: "It is not a mere possible doubt; because everything relating to human affairs, and depending on moral evidence is open to some possible or imaginary doubt. It is that state of the case, which, after the entire comparison and consideration of all the evidence, leaves the minds of jurors in that condition that they cannot say they feel an abiding conviction, to a moral certainty, of the truth of the charge. [C.P.C., sec. 1096]

Some instructions are quotations taken from the opinions of previous cases. In California there is a printed set of instructions that is widely used both by the prosecution and the defense. These are instructions which have been used before and have been upheld on appeal. The work is CAL JIC* and has been prepared by the Los Angeles Supreme Court. These, for example, are general instructions that set forth the functions of the court and the jury:

> You are the exclusive judges of the facts and of the effect and value of the evidence, but you must determine the facts from the evidence produced here in court. If any evidence was admitted and afterwards was ordered by me to be stricken out, you must disregard entirely the matter thus stricken, and if any counsel intimated by any of his questions that certain hinted facts were, or were not, true, you must disregard any such intimation, and must not draw any inference from it. As to any statement made by counsel in your presence concerning the facts in the case, you must not regard such a statement as evidence; provided, however, that if counsel for all parties have

* California Jury Instructions, Criminal, rev. ed.

stipulated to any fact, you are to regard that fact as being conclusively proved; and if, in the trial, any party has admitted a fact to be true, such admission may be considered by you as evidence in the case.

It is the duty of the jurors to deliberate and consult with a view of reaching an agreement, if they can do so without violence to their individual judgment, upon the evidence, under the instructions of the Court. Each juror must decide the case for himself, but should do so only after a consideration of the case with his fellow jurors, and he should not hesitate to change his views or opinions on the case when convinced that they are erroneous. No juror should vote for either side nor be influenced in so voting for the single reason that a majority of the jury should be in favor of such party. In other words, despite your duty to agree if such be possible, you should not surrender your honest convictions concerning the effect or weight of evidence nor violate your duty to give the defendant the benefit of any reasonable doubt you may entertain as to his guilt for the mere purpose of returning a verdict for or against either side solely because of the opinion of the other jurors. Your verdict must be unanimous.

Once the jury has been instructed, they retire to the jury room and deliberate.

Erroneous Instructions. One of the most common grounds of appeal is an erroneous instruction. If the court reads an instruction that mistakes the law, the trial will be reversed. The error itself must be of some substance, however, and a mere typographical error will not be grounds for reversal unless, of course, it affects the main substance of the instruction.

Rereading of Instructions. Once the jury has left the courtroom and begun its deliberation, the court recesses until a verdict has been reached. It frequently happens that the jury will want to be instructed again upon a certain phase of the trial. The jury must be reconvened and assembled in the jury box in order to hear an instruction again. It is considered poor procedure to give

the trial

the written instruction to the jurors in the jury room. They usually are reinstructed orally on any points that they wish reviewed. Section 1138 of the Penal Code provides:

> After the jury have retired for deliberation, if there be any disagreement between them as to the testimony, or if they desire to be informed on any point of law arising in the case, they must require the officer to conduct them into court. Upon being brought into court, the information required must be given in the presence of, or after notice to, the prosecuting attorney, and the defendant or his counsel, or after they have been called.

Deliberation. Once the case has been presented, the final arguments concluded, and the instructions read to the jury, the jury retires to the jury room and deliberates the case in order to reach a verdict. Prior to retiring to the jury room, the jurors are told by the judge ". . . that it is their duty not to converse among themselves or with anyone else on any subject connected with the trial, or to form or express any opinion thereon until the cause is finally submitted to them." (C.P.C., sec. 1122)

A court officer, usually the bailiff, has custody of the jurors while they are deliberating. He, of course, is not present but ensures that their deliberations are private and in secret. He must also see that they do not speak to any other persons and that he in no way communicates or speaks to them himself without an order of the court. Penal Code section 1128 states: ". . . an officer must be sworn to keep them together in some private and convenient place, and not to permit any person to speak to or communicate with them, nor to do so himself, unless by order of the court, or to ask them whether they have agreed upon a verdict, and to return them into court when they have so agreed or when ordered by the court."

The jurors may take with them all papers which have been received into evidence. Although the Penal Code section allowing papers to be taken into evidence mentions only papers, exhibits that have been received into evidence may also be taken into the jury room (C.P.C., sec. 1137).

The jury must be left together while deliberating. They must not be separated into groups unless they are "locked up for the night," in which case the male and the female jurors are separated. The courts go to great lengths to enforce the rules of keeping the jurors together while deliberating. In *People v. Thornton*, 74 Cal. 483 (1888), several of the jurors went to a bar for drinks while at the restaurant they were taken to for dinner, and the court held that this raised a presumption of prejudice.

The jurors must reach a verdict before they can be discharged. Their verdict must be unanimous, i.e., 12 for guilty or 12 for acquittal. If it becomes apparent that a verdict cannot be reached within a reasonable time, the judge may discharge the jury. This is referred to as a "hung jury," i.e., one which cannot reach a verdict. The judge must feel that there is no reasonable probability that the jury can agree before the jury may be discharged. There is no set time limit as to when it is unreasonable for the court to release the jurors without a verdict, although it would seem that at least four to five hours should elapse in deliberation before it would appear that the jury cannot reach a verdict.

THE VERDICT

The "verdict" is defined by *Black's Law Dictionary*, third edition, as "the formal and unanimous decision or finding made by a jury impanelled and sworn for the trial of a cause and reported to the court, and accepted by it upon the matters or questions duly submitted to them upon the trial." The verdict is generally written on a form which has been provided by the court. There is no requirement, however, for verdicts to be written.

The defendant must be present for the verdict in felony cases. There is an exception when the defendant cannot be found after due diligence; in the interest of justice the court may render the verdict (C.P.C., sec. 1148). The defendant need not be present for the verdict in misdemeanor cases.

The jury is asked by the court or clerk whether it has agreed upon a verdict, and if it has, the verdict must be declared.

General Verdict. A general verdict is either "not guilty" or "guilty," i.e., one which denotes either acquittal or conviction. When there has been a separate trial on a plea of insanity, the jury returns a verdict either of "sane at the time the offense was committed" or "insane at the time the offense was committed." (C.P.C., secs. 1151 and 1026)

Special Verdict. A "special verdict" is one in which the jury finds the *facts only*, leaving the judgment up to the court. It may be rendered only in Superior Court, for any matter except libel, and is rendered when the jury is in doubt as to the legal effect of the facts. A special verdict must be in writing or entered in the minutes of the court and read to the jury and agreed by them before they can be discharged (C.P.C., secs. 1150, 1152, and 1153).

Degree. Penal Code section 1157 states that "Whenever a defendant is convicted of a crime which is distinguished into degrees, the jury, or the court if a jury trial is waived, must find the degree of the crime of which he is guilty. Upon the failure of the jury or the court to so determine, the degree of the crime of which the defendant is guilty, shall be deemed to be of the lesser degree."

Previous Offenses. If the defendant is also charged with a previous offense in the accusatory pleadings and he is found guilty of the offense charged, the jury must find whether or not the defendant has suffered the previous convictions. The jury need not make such a determination if the defendant admits the previous offense (C.P.C., sec. 1158).

Two or More Defendants. Section 1160 of the Penal Code states that

> On a charge against two or more defendants jointly, if the jury cannot agree upon a verdict as to all, they may render a verdict as to the defendant or defendants in regard to whom they do agree, on which a judgment must be entered accordingly, and the case as to the other may be tried again.
>
> Where two or more offenses are charged in an accusatory pleading, if the jury cannot agree upon a verdict as to all of them, they may render a verdict as to the charge or charges upon which they do agree, and the charges on which they do not agree may be tried again.

Lesser Offenses and Attempts. The jury may find the defendant guilty of any offenses that are included offenses of the crime charged, or it may return a verdict of guilty of an attempt to commit the crime (C.P.C., sec. 1159).

Recommendations and Correction of the Verdict. Where the jury returns a verdict of guilty and it appears to the court that the jury is mistaken on the law, the court may explain why a mistake exists and direct the jury to reconvene and reconsider the verdict. If the jury still returns the same verdict, the verdict will be entered. However, the court may not direct a reconsideration when the verdict is an acquittal. If the defendant is acquitted, he must be released from custody. If the defendant is found guilty, he must be remanded to the custody of the sheriff or other officer of the county to await the judgment of the court upon the verdict (C.P.C., sec. 1166).

Recommendation of Sentencing. There is no authorized verdict for sentencing of the defendant. If the jury so recommends, the judge may disregard such a recommendation or consider it.

SUMMARY

A jury trial is commenced after the jury has been selected by the prosecution and defense. The selection of jurors consists of questioning to determine their qualifications to act in an impartial manner. The two types of challenge for jurors are peremptory, for which no reason for excusing the witness may be given, and for cause, which is usually related to some form of bias on the part of the prospective juror. A defendant charged with an offense punishable by death or life imprisonment is entitled to twenty peremptory challenges. For all other offenses the defendant is entitled to ten peremptory challenges.

The prosecutor in a criminal action is usually the district attorney. A prosecutor has discretion as to whether or not to file a criminal complaint. A public defender may be appointed to defend an indigent defendant.

The stages of a trial are as follows: Prosecution presents its case. Defense presents its case. Prosecution may offer rebuttal evidence. Defense may offer rebuttal evidence. Prosecution presents final argument. Defense presents final argument, and then prosecution presents closing argument. Once the case is argued, the judge instructs the jury on the law. The jury deliberates and returns a verdict. The jury is then dismissed, and the trial is ended.

QUESTIONS

1. What is the "order of the trial"? What is the sequence of events after the swearing in of the jury?
2. What are the qualifications of a juror?
3. What is the distinction between a challenge for cause and a peremptory challenge?
4. A general challenge for cause is broken down into two categories. What are they? How do they differ?

5. On what basis may being a party adverse to the defendant in a civil action be challenged?
6. Why does the defense attorney repeatedly emphasize the presumption of innocence during his questioning of the jury?
7. Who makes the final decision as to questions of bias of a juror?
8. What is the number of peremptory challenges when the offense is one punishable by death?
9. What is the prosecutor's role in the trial? The defense attorney's role?
10. What is the public defender system?
11. What matters are usually contained in the opening statements? Does the defense usually make an opening statement?
12. What are the types of objections made at a trial?
13. What is the order of presentation of evidence at a trial?
14. Why is a final argument important to the prosecution? To the defense?
15. What information is contained in instructions to the jury?
16. What discretion does the judge have in regard to instructions submitted to him?
17. What are the sources for instructions?
18. What is the effect of an erroneous instruction?
19. Under what circumstances is the jury "locked up for the night"?
20. What are the types of verdicts?

8

post-trial proceedings

POST-TRIAL AND PREJUDGMENT PROCEDURE

We may say that post-trial proceedings begin immediately after the verdict has been found. Popular belief that the court proceeding, in any given case, is essentially terminated with the finding of a verdict is certainly a misunderstood concept. As we progress in the study of post-trial proceedings we shall see that this point is but a beginning for many criminal cases. Obviously, if a verdict of *not guilty* is returned or the defendant is exonerated of guilt by other means, the proceedings will conclude. If, however, he is found guilty or has pleaded guilty and is held to receive judgment, another complete set of procedures is called into play. California Penal Code section 1191 states:

> In the Superior Court, after a plea, finding or verdict of guilty, or after a finding or verdict against the defendant on a plea of a former conviction or acquittal, or once in jeopardy, the Court must appoint a time for pronouncing judgment, which must be within 21 days after the verdict, finding or plea of guilty, during which time the Court shall refer the case to the

probation officer for a report if eligible to probation and pursuant to section 1203 of this code; provided, however, that the Court may extend the time not more than 10 days for the purpose of hearing or determining any motion for a new trial, or in arrest of judgment, and may further extend the time until the probation officer's report is received and until any proceedings for granting or denying probation have been disposed of. If in the opinion of the Court there is reasonable ground of believing a defendant insane, the Court may extend the time for pronouncing sentence until the question of insanity has been heard and determined, as provided in this code. If the Court orders defendant placed in a diagnostic facility pursuant to Section 1203.03, the time otherwise allowed by this section for pronouncing judgment is extended by a period equal to (1) the number of days which elapse between the date of such order and the date on which notice is received from the Director of Corrections advising whether or not the Department of Correction will receive defendant in such facility, and (2) if the director notifies the Court that it will receive the defendant, the time which elapses until his return to the Court from the facility.

It is obvious that the time limit of twenty-one days from verdict to judgment is designed to prompt the court and the defendant to carry out their business without unwarranted delay—the court in imposing judgment and the defendant in making his possible motions for a new trial. This limitation is certainly not to be enforced in such a manner as to endanger the legal processes.

Immediately after the verdict is found, the court will appoint a date for judgment. This date may be any day within the twenty-one-day limit, and its setting is entirely within the discretion of the court. This does not mean, however, that in any given case the judgment will be pronounced on that date. The following variables provide great flexibility in the final disposition of the case.

Referral to Probation Officer. Directly following the setting of a date for the pronouncing of judgment, the court will refer the case to the probation officer if the defendant is eligible for probation pursuant to section 1203 of the Penal Code. (We shall discuss probation in more detail later on in this chapter.) In any event, the time limit may be extended until the probation report is returned to the court.

Hearings and Determinations on Motions for a New Trial. The court may also extend the time limit for more than ten days in order to hear and determine motions for a new trial or in arrest of judgment.

Question of Insanity and Commitment to a Diagnostic Facility. If the question of insanity arises, the court may elect to determine such a question and is authorized to extend the time limit in order to do so. If the court acts under Penal Code section 1203.03 and orders the defendant to a diagnostic facility for mental examination, the time limit must be extended to cover the period needed for placement by the Department of Corrections, as well as a period (not exceeding ninety days) for the diagnostic examination itself. Section 1203.03 of the Penal Code provides that if in a felony case the court concludes that a just determination of the case requires such diagnosis and treatment as can be afforded at a diagnostic facility of the Department of Corrections, it may order the defendant to be placed in such facility for a period not to exceed ninety days. Within this period the director of the Department of Corrections is to report his diagnosis and recommendations, and the defendant will then either be returned to the court or placed in the proper facility. No defendant can be transported to any such facility until the director has notified the court of the place to which such person is to be transported and the time at which he can be received.

MOTIONS FOR A NEW TRIAL AND IN ARREST OF JUDGMENT

A motion in arrest of judgment will stay the pronouncement of judgment if it legally qualifies under Penal Code section 1201, which specifies:

> He may show, for cause against the judgment:
> 1. That he is insane; and if, in the opinion of the Court, there is reasonable ground for believing him insane, the question of insanity must be tried as provided in chapter six, title ten, part two of this code. If, upon the trial of that question, the jury finds that he is sane, judgment must be pronounced, but if they find him insane, he must be committed to the state hospital for the care and treatment of the insane, until he becomes sane; and when notice is given of that fact, as provided in section one thousand three hundred and seventy-two, he must be brought before the Court for judgment;
> 2. That he has good cause to offer, either in arrest of judgment or for a new trial; in which case the Court may, in its discretion, order the judgment to be deferred, and proceed to decide upon the motion in arrest of judgment or for a new trial.

The grounds for a motion in arrest of judgment are outlined in Penal Code section 1185, which generally defines the motion as an application on the part of the defendant that no judgment be rendered and that a determination be made before the judgment is pronounced. Also, pursuant to Penal Code section 1186, the judge may arrest the judgment on his own motion: "The Court may, on its own motion, at any time before judgment is pronounced, arrest the judgment for any of the defects in the accusatory pleading [see Penal Code section 1004] upon which a motion in arrest of judgment may be founded as provided in Section 1185, by order for that purpose entered upon its minutes."

Penal Code section 1201.5 adds:

Any motions made subsequent to judgment must be made only upon written notice served upon the prosecution at least three days prior to the date of hearing thereon. No affidavit or other writing shall be presented or considered in support thereof unless a copy of the same has been duly served upon the prosecution at least three days prior to a hearing thereon. Any appeal from an order entered upon a motion made other than as herein provided, must be dismissed by the Court.

The effect of an order arresting judgment is outlined as follows in Penal Code section 1187: "The effect of an order arresting judgment, in a Superior Court, is to place the defendant in the same situation in which he was immediately before the indictment was found or information filed. In any other Court the effect is to place the defendant in the situation in which he was before the trial was had."

A motion for a new trial may also be made at this point in the proceedings. In this case, the motion must be made by the defendant, as the court does not have the power to make such a motion of its own volition. It may be more properly stated that the court has no authority to grant a new trial of its own motion. The trial court does, however, have sole discretion in the granting or denial of such a motion.

The following are the Penal Code sections which outline the statutory procedure for a motion for a new trial:

> A new trial is re-examination of the issue in the same Court, before another jury, after a verdict has been given. [C.P.C., sec. 1179]

> The granting of a new trial places the parties in the same position as if no trial had been had. All the testimony must be produced anew, and the former verdict or finding cannot be used or referred to, either in evidence or in argument, or be pleaded in bar of any conviction which might have been had under the accusatory pleading. [C.P.C., sec. 1180]

> When a verdict has been rendered or a finding made against the defendant, the Court may, upon his application, grant a new trial, in the following cases only:

1. When the trial has been had in his absence, except in cases where the trial may lawfully proceed in his absence;
2. When the jury has received an evidence out of Court, other than that resulting from a view of the premises, or of personal property;
3. When the jury has separated without leave of the Court after retiring to deliberate upon their verdict, or been guilty of any misconduct by which a fair and due consideration of the case has been prevented;
4. When the verdict has been decided by lot, or by any means other than a fair expression of opinion on the part of all the jurors;
5. When the Court has misdirected the jury in a matter of law, or has erred in the decision of any question of law arising during the course of the trial, and when the District Attorney or other counsel prosecuting the case has been guilty of prejudicial misconduct during the trial thereof before a jury;
6. When the verdict or finding is contrary to law or evidence, but if the evidence shows the defendant to be not guilty of the degree of the crime of which he was convicted, but guilty of a lesser degree thereof, or of a lesser crime included therein, the Court may modify the verdict, finding or judgment accordingly without granting or ordering a new trial, and this power shall extend to any Court to which the cause may be appealed;
7. When the verdict or finding is contrary to law or evidence, but in any case wherein authority is vested by statute in the trial Court or jury to recommend or determine as a part of its verdict or finding the punishment to be imposed, the Court may modify such verdict or finding by imposing the lesser punishment without granting or ordering a new trial, and this power shall extend to any Court to which the case may be appealed;
8. When new evidence is discovered material to the defendant, and which he could not, with reasonable diligence, have discovered and produced at the trial. When a motion for a new trial is made upon the ground of newly discovered evidence, the defendant must produce at the hearing, in sup-

port thereof, the affidavits of the witnesses by whom such evidence is expected to be given, and if time is required by the defendant to procure such affidavits, the Court may postpone the hearing of the motion for such length of time as, under all circumstances of the case, may seem reasonable. [C.P.C., sec. 1181]

The application for a new trial must be made and determined before judgment or the making of an order granting probation, the commitment of a defendant for observation as a mentally disordered sex offender, or the commitment of a defendant for narcotics addiction or insanity, whichever first occurs, and the order granting or denying such application must be immediately entered by the clerk in the minutes. [C.P.C., sec. 1182]

There are certainly many varied points of law to be considered within the realm of a motion for a new trial. Most of these points, except for the statutory procedural rules, are not pertinent to our study. However, an interesting and important element to any peace officer testifying in a criminal trial arises from subsection 5 of Penal Code section 1181, which holds that prejudicial misconduct may extend to a witness who in some way prejudices the jury by his testimony. A case in point is taken from Fricke, *California Criminal Procedures:* *

> When in testifying to a conversation with the defendant, a police officer included the statement that he had also questioned the defendant about his activities some years prior, when he was a suspect in another case in which the defendant denied the accusation, the Court, on the theory that the officer's misconduct was deliberate and with the idea of prejudicing the defendant, held that this was prejudicial error for which the trial Judge should have granted the defendant's request for a mistrial. [*People v. Bentley*, 131 Cal. App. 2d 687 (1955)]

* Charles W. Fricke, *California Criminal Procedure*, 6th ed., Legal Book Store, Los Angeles, 1962, pp. 435, 436.

SEXUAL PSYCHOPATH PROCEEDINGS

Sections 6300 to 6326 of the California Welfare and Institutions Code (C.W.I.C.) govern the legal procedure applying to the sexual psychopathy of the suspected criminal. This procedure is correctly invoked after a conviction and before the imposition of sentence or the placement of probation. Although the trial is criminal in nature, it is interesting that the sexual psychopath proceedings have been held to be civil, but are collateral to such criminal trial.

The legal provisions relating to sexual psychopath proceedings are as follows:

> As used in this article, "mentally disordered sex offender" means any person who by reason of mental defect, disease, or disorder, is predisposed to the commission of sexual offenses to such a degree that he is dangerous to the health and safety of others. Wherever the term "sexual psychopath" is used in any code, such term shall be construed to refer to and mean a "mentally disordered sex offender." [C.W.I.C., sec. 6300]
>
> (a) When a person is convicted of any criminal offense, whether or not a sex offense, the trial Judge, on his own motion, or on motion of the prosecuting attorney, or on application by affidavit by or on behalf of the defendant, if it appears to the satisfaction of the Court that there is probable cause for believing such a person is a mentally disordered sex offender within the meaning of this chapter, may adjourn the proceeding or suspend the sentence, as the case may be, and may certify the person for hearing and examination by the Superior Court of the county to determine whether the person is a mentally disordered sex offender within the meaning of this chapter. Conviction upon a charge of violation of Section 290 of the Penal Code by failure to register as required thereby is conviction of a criminal offense within the meaning of this subdivision.

(b) When a person is convicted of a sex offense involving a child under 14 years of age and it is a misdemeanor, and the person has been previously convicted of a sex offense in this or any other state, the Court shall adjourn the proceeding or suspend the sentence, as the case may be, and shall certify the person for hearing and examination by the Superior Court of the county to determine whether the person is a mentally disordered sex offender within the meaning of this chapter.

(c) When a person is convicted of a sex offense involving a child under 14 years of age and it is a felony, the Court shall adjourn the proceeding or suspend the sentence, as the case may be, and shall certify the person for hearing and examination by the Superior Court of the county to determine whether the person is a mentally disordered sex offender within the meaning of this chapter.

(d) When a person over the age of 16 years has been found by the Juvenile Court to be a person described by Section 601 or 602 of this code and adjudged to be a ward of the Court, the Juvenile Court Judge on his own motion, or on motion of the probation officer, or on application by or on behalf of the ward, if it appears to the satisfaction of the Court that there is probable cause for believing such person is a mentally disordered sex offender within the meaning of this chapter, may adjourn the proceeding and may certify the person for hearing and examination by the Superior Court of the county to determine whether the person is a mentally disordered sex offender within the meaning of this chapter. [(a)–(d), C.W.I.C., sec. 6302]

When an affidavit is filed under (a) or (d) it shall be substantially in the form specified for the affidavit of mental illness in Section 5049 of this code except that the title and body of the affidavit shall refer to such person as "an alleged mentally disordered sex offender" and shall state fully the facts upon which the allegation that the person is a mentally disordered sex offender is based. If the person is then before the Court or is in custody, the Court may order that the person be detained in a place of safety until the issue and service of a warrant of apprehension as provided by this chapter.

When the Court certifies the person for hearing and examination by the Superior Court of the county to determine whether the person is a mentally disordered sex offender, the Court shall transmit to the Superior Court its certification to that effect, accompanied by a statement of the Court's reasons for finding that there is probable cause for believing such a person is a mentally disordered sex offender within the meaning of this chapter in cases certified under (a) or (d), or a statement of the facts making such certification mandatory under (b) or (c).

The Judge or Justice presiding in such Court, whenever it is deemed necessary or advisable, may issue and deliver to some peace officer for service, a warrant directing that the person be apprehended and taken before a Judge of the Superior Court for a hearing and examination to determine whether the person is a mentally disordered sex offender. The officer shall thereupon apprehend and detain the person until a hearing and examination can be had. At the time of the apprehension a copy of the affidavit if one was filed, the certification, accompanied by the Court's statement, and the warrant shall be personally delivered to the person and copies thereof shall also be delivered to the Superior Court to which the person was certified and to the District Attorney of the county.

The warrant of apprehension shall be substantially in the form provided by Section 5050.1 of this code for the apprehension of a person alleged to be mentally ill. [C.W.I.C., sec. 6252]

The person certified or alleged to be a mentally disordered sex offender shall be taken before a Judge of the Superior Court of the county. The Judge shall then inform him that he is certified or alleged to be a mentally disordered sex offender, and inform him of his rights to make a reply and to produce witnesses in relation thereto. The Judge shall by order fix such time and place for the hearing and examination in open Court as will give reasonable opportunity for the filing of the probation officer's report as provided in Section 5503.5, and for the production and examination of witnesses. If, however, the person is too ill to appear in Court, or if appearance in Court would be detrimental to the mental or physical health of the person, the Judge may hold the hearing at the bedside of the person. The order shall be entered at length in the minute book of the Court or shall be signed by the Judge and filed, and a certified copy thereof served on the person. The Judge shall order that notice of the apprehension of the person and of the hearing of mentally disordered sex offender be served on the District Attorney of the county and on such relatives of the person known to be residing in the County as the Judge deems necessary or proper.

If the alleged mentally disordered sex offender has no attorney the Judge may appoint an attorney to represent him, or if a request is made for an attorney by the alleged mentally disordered sex offender, the Judge shall appoint an attorney to represent him, and, in a county where there is no public defender, fix the compensation to be paid by the county for such services if the Court determines that the person is not financially able to employ counsel. [C.W.I.C., sec. 6305]

The Court shall refer the matter to the probation officer, along with a copy of the certification accompanied by the certifying Court's statement, and the name and address of each psychiatrist appointed pursuant to Section 5504, to investigate and report to the Court within a specified time upon the circumstances surrounding the crime and the prior record and history of the person. The report shall include the criminal record, if any, of the person, obtained from the State Bureau of Criminal Identification and Investigation. The probation officer shall furnish to the psychiatrists pertinent information concerning the circumstances surrounding the crime and the prior record and history of the person. [C.W.I.C., sec. 6306]

The Judge shall appoint not less than two nor more than three psychiatrists, each of whom shall be a holder of a valid and unrevoked physician's and surgeon's certificate who has directed his professional practice primarily to the diagnosis and treatment of mental and nervous disorders for a period of not less than five years, and at least one of whom shall be from the medical staff of a state hospital or county psychopathic hospital, to make a personal examination of the alleged mentally disordered sex offender, directed toward ascertaining whether the person is a mentally disordered sex offender. [C.W.I.C., sec. 6307]

Each psychiatrist so appointed shall file with the Court a separate written report of the result of his examination, together with his conclusions and recommendations and his opinion as to whether or not the person would benefit by care and treatment in a state hospital. At the hearing each psychiatrist shall hear the testimony of all witnesses, and shall testify as to the result of his examination and to any other pertinent facts within his knowledge, unless the person upon the advice of counsel waives the presence of the psychiatrists and it is stipulated that their respective reports may be received in evidence. [C.W.I.C., sec. 6308]

Any psychiatrist so appointed by the Court may be called by either party to the proceeding or by the Court itself and when so called shall be subject to all legal objections as to competency and bias and as to qualification as an expert. When called by the Court, or by either party to the proceeding, the Court may examine the psychiatrist, as deemed necessary, but either party shall have the same right to object to the questions asked by the Court and the evidence adduced as though the psychiatrist were a witness for the adverse party. When the psychiatrist is called and examined by the Court the parties may cross-examine him in the order directed by the Court. When called by either party to the proceeding the adverse party may examine him the same as in the case of any other witness called by such party. [C.W.I.C., sec. 6309]

The psychiatrists so appointed by the Court shall be allowed such fees as in the discretion of the Court seem just and reasonable, with regard to the services rendered by the psychiatrists, but in no event shall such fees exceed the sum of forty dollars ($40) per day in addition to actual traveling expenses. The fees allowed shall be paid by the county in which the hearing is held. [C.W.I.C., sec. 6310]

The provisions of this article relating to psychiatrists appointed by the Court shall not be deemed or construed to prevent any party to a proceeding under this article from producing any other expert evidence as to the mental condition of the alleged mentally disordered sex offender. [C.W.I.C., sec. 6311]

The Judge shall also cause to be examined as a witness any other person whom he believes to have knowledge of the mental condition of the alleged mentally disordered sex offender, or the financial condition of the alleged mentally disordered sex offender and of any person liable for his support. [C.W I.C., sec. 6312]

The Judge may, for any hearing, order the clerk of the Court to issue subpoenas and compel the attendance of witnesses from any place within the boundaries of this state; but no person is obliged to attend as a witness in such a hearing out of the county where he resides or is served unless the Judge, upon affidavit to the effect that affiant believes that the evidence of the witness is material and his attendance at the hearing necessary, indorses on the subpoena an order for the attendance of the witness.

All witnesses, other than psychiatrists appointed by the Court, attending a hearing upon a subpoena issued under this section shall be entitled to the same fees and expenses as in criminal cases, to be paid upon the same conditions and in like manner. [C.W.I.C., sec. 6313]

The alleged mentally disordered sex offender shall be present at the hearing, and if he has no attorney, the Judge may appoint an attorney to represent him, or the Judge may order the county Public Defender to represent him at the hearing, if he determines that the person is not financially able to employ counsel. [C.W.I.C., sec. 6314]

If, upon the hearing, the person is found by the Superior Court not to be a mentally disordered sex offender, the Superior Court shall return the person to the Court in which the case originated for such disposition as that Court may deem necessary and proper.

If the Court finds the person is a mentally disordered sex offender, but would not benefit by care and treatment in a state hospital, the Court may return the person to the Court in which the case originated for such disposition as that Court may deem necessary and proper. [C.W.I.C., sec. 6315]

If, after examination and hearing, it appears there is sufficient cause to believe that the person is a mentally disordered sex offender within the meaning of this article, the Judge may make and sign an order that the person be placed temporarily in a suitable psychiatric facility maintained by a county or in a state hospital of the Department of Mental Hygiene designated by the Court for observation and diagnosis for a period not to exceed 90 days, with the further provision in said order that the superintendent of the hospital or person in charge of the county facility shall report to the Court the diagnosis and recommendations concerning such person within the 90-day period. The Court shall attach to the order for observation its findings and copies of the certification and statement from the other Court, any affidavits filed, the written reports of the Court-appointed psychiatrists, and the report of the probation officer, together with such social and other data that it has available bearing upon the case, and the same shall be delivered to the institution with such order.

The superintendent of the hospital or person in charge of the county facility shall within 90 days cause the person to be examined and forward to the committing Court his opinion as to whether or not the person is a mentally disordered sex offender, whether or not he is a danger to the health and safety of others, and whether or not he will benefit by care and treatment in a state hospital, including therein a report, diagnosis and recommendation concerning the person's future care, supervision and treatment.

If the superintendent of the hospital or person in charge of the county facility reports to the Court that the person is not a mentally disordered sex offender, the person shall be returned to the Court for further disposition of his case. The Court shall then cause the person to be returned to the Court in which the criminal charge was tried to await further action with reference to such criminal charge.

If the superintendent of the hospital or person in charge of the county facility reports to the committing Court that the person is a mentally disordered sex offender but will not benefit by care or treatment in a state hospital and is a danger to the health and safety of others, the Court shall then cause the person to be returned to the Court in which the criminal charge was tried to await further action with reference to such criminal charge. Such Court shall resume the proceedings and shall impose sentence or make such other suitable disposition of the case as the Court deems necessary. If, however, such Court is satisfied that the person is a mentally disordered sex offender but would not benefit by care or treatment in a state hospital and is a danger to the health and safety of others, it may recertify the person to the Superior Court of the county. If the Superior Court, after hearing, finds that the person is a mentally disordered sex offender but would not benefit by care or treatment in a state hospital and is a danger to the health and safety of others, it may make an order committing the person for an indefinite period to the Department of Mental Hygiene for placement in a state institution or institutional unit for the care and treatment of mentally disordered sex offenders designated by the Court and provided pursuant to Section 6326. At such hearing or hearings, the person shall be entitled to present witnesses in his own behalf, to be represented by counsel and to cross-examine any witnesses who testify against him. The person shall remain in such institution or institutional unit until he is no longer a danger to the health and safety of others. Thereupon, the proceedings set forth in Section 6325 shall be followed with respect to the certifying of an opinion to the committing Court and the release of the person thereby.

If the superintendent of the hospital or person in charge of the county facility reports to the Court that the person is a mentally disordered sex offender and that the person could benefit by treatment in a state hospital, the Court in its discretion has the alternative to return the person to the criminal Court for further disposition or may make an order committing the person to the department for placement in a state hospital for an indeterminate period and a copy of such commitment shall be personally served upon said person within five days after the making of such order and such person may within 10 days demand a hearing in Court and upon such demand said Court shall order the return of said person to said Court and fix a time and place for a hearing. Upon such hearing the Court may accept the report of the superintendent of the hospital or person in charge of the county facility, if verified, in lieu of the examination by and testimony of Court-appointed psychiatrists, or may consider the report as additional evidence. Upon such further hearing the Court may make an order committing the person to the department for placement in a state hospital designated by the Court for an indeterminate period, or may make other suitable disposition of the case.

No person shall be committed for an indeterminate period as a mentally disordered sex offender unless an observation placement has been made and reported, diagnosed and recommended upon as provided by this section. [C.W.I.C., sec. 6316]

If the Court orders the commitment of the person to the department for placement in a state hospital for an indeterminate period, the Court may, in the order of commitment, require the superintendent of the state hospital to make periodic reports to the Court concerning the person's progress towards recovery. [C.W.I.C., sec. 6317]

The sheriff of any county wherein an order is made by the Court committing a person for an indeterminate period to a state hospital or returning such person to the Court, or any other peace officer designated by the Court, shall execute the writ of commitment or order of return, and receive as compensation therefor such fees as are now or may hereafter be provided by law for the transportation of prisoners to the state prison, which shall be payable in the same manner. No female person committed pursuant to this article shall be taken to or from any state or other hospital without the attendance of some woman of good character and mature age or of a relative of the person.

The expense of transporting a person to a county facility or state hospital temporarily for an observation placement under this article and returning such person to the Court is a charge upon the county in which the Court is situated. [C.W.I.C., sec. 6322]

Certified copies of the affidavit, certification from the trial Court, warrant of apprehension, order for hearing and examination, report of the probation officer and of the Court-appointed psychiatrists, and the order of placement for observation or order of commitment for an indeterminate period, as the case may be, shall be delivered to the person transporting the mentally disordered sex offender to the county facility or state hospital, and shall be delivered by that person to the officer in charge of the facility or hospital. [C.W.I.C., sec. 6323]

The provisions of Section 4025 and Article 4 relative to the property and support of mentally ill persons and inebriates in state hospitals, the liability for such support, and the powers and duties of the Department of Mental Hygiene and all officers and employees thereof in connection therewith shall apply to persons committed to state hospitals pursuant to this article the same as if such persons were expressly referred to in said Section 4025. [C.W.I.C., sec. 6324]

Whenever a person who is committed for an indeterminate period to the department for placement in a state hospital as a mentally disordered sex offender (a) has been treated to such an extent that in the opinion of the superintendent the person will not benefit by further care and treatment in the hospital and is not a danger to the health and safety of others, or (b) has not recovered, and in the opinion of the superintendent the person is still a danger to the health and safety of others, the superintendent of the hospital shall file with the committing Court a certification of his opinion under (a) or (b), as the case may be, including therein a report, diagnosis and recommendation concerning the person's future care, supervision or treatment. If the opinion so certified is under (a) the committing Court shall forthwith order the return of the person to said committing Court and shall thereafter cause the person to be returned to the Court in which the criminal charge was tried to await further action with reference to such criminal charge.

Such Court shall resume the proceedings, upon the return of the person to the Court, and after considering all the evidence before it may place the person on probation for a period of not less than five years if the criminal charge permits such probation and the person is otherwise eligible for probation. As a condition of such probation the person shall totally abstain from the use of alcoholic liquor or beverages. In any case, where the person is sentenced on a criminal charge, the time the person spent under indeterminate commitment as a mentally disordered sex offender shall be credited in fixing his term of sentence. [C.W.I.C., sec. 6325]

If the opinion so certified is under subdivision (b) of Section 6325, the committing Court shall forthwith order the return of the person to said committing Court and shall thereafter cause the person to be returned to the Court in which the criminal charge was tried to await further action with reference to such criminal charge.

Such Court shall resume the proceedings and after considering all the evidence before it shall impose sentence or make such other disposition of the case as the Court may deem necessary and proper; provided that said Court, if satisfied that the person has not recovered from his mental disorder and is still a danger to the health and safety of others, may recertify the person to the Superior Court of the county. If said Court after hearing makes a finding that the person is still a mentally disordered sex offender and is still a danger to the health and safety of others, it may make an order recommitting the person for an indeterminate period to the Department of Mental Hygiene for placement in a state institution or institutional unit for the care and treatment of such mentally disordered sex offenders designated by the Court. At such hearing or hearings, the person shall be entitled to present witnesses in his own behalf, to be represented by counsel and to cross-examine any witnesses who testify against him.

The Director of Mental Hygiene, with the approval of the Director of Corrections and the Director of Finance, may provide on the grounds of a state institution or institutions under the jurisdiction of the Department of Corrections or the Department of Mental Hygiene one or more institutional units to be used for the custodial care and treatment of mentally disordered sex offenders. Each such unit shall be administered in the manner provided by law for the government of the institution in which such unit is established.

The Court shall cause the person so recommitted to be delivered to the state institution or the institutional unit so designated. The person shall remain therein or in any other such institution or institutional unit to which he may be transferred by the Director of Mental Hygiene until the person is no longer a danger to the health and safety of others. Thereupon the proceedings set forth in Section 5517 shall be followed with respect to the certifying of an opinion to the committing Court and the release of the person thereby. [C.W.I.C., sec. 6326]

In *People v. McCracken*, 39 Cal. 2d 336–346 (1952), we find the substantiating authority for the physical removal from society of the sexual psychopath. It is well established that a sexual psychopath may be removed from society until cured or at least considered to be safe for release. However, the case also points out that "the Court may thereafter resume the criminal proceedings and impose the punishment allowed by law since the confinement as a sexual psychopath is not a substitute for punishment."

It is important that the definition of "sexual psychopath" not be misconstrued or misunderstood. The definition is clearly stated in section 6300 and in no way implies that the sexual psychopath must be or is considered insane. "Criminal insanity" is an entirely different legal concept, and the two should not be confused. [See *People v. Tipton*, 90 Cal. App. 2d 103 (1949).] It is also clearly held that a person who is sexually perverted should not be automatically considered a sexual psychopath under the law. [See *People v. Parish*, 75 Cal. App. 2d 907 (1946).]

SUMMARY

Immediately after a guilty verdict has been found, post-trial proceedings begin. A period of twenty-one days is provided before pronouncing of judgment, and during such time the court refers the case to the probation officer for a presentence investigation. There are, however, provisions for extending the time limit to cover hearings that may be requested on motions for a new trial or to determine sanity.

In such cases as when the defendant is found to be insane, he is committed to a state hospital until such time as he can again be brought before the court for judgment. In cases where an order for the arrest of judgment is found, a defendant in Superior Court will be in the same position as he was before the indictment or information was found; in any other court, he will be in the same situation as he was before the trial was held.

If the defendant is granted a new trial, this places the parties in the same position as if no trial had been held at all.

There are eight instances in which the court may, upon the application of the defendant, grant a new trial.

A special proceeding may be heard in the case of a mentally disordered sex offender who, when so adjudged, will be placed in a diagnostic facility for ninety days to determine the extent and treatability of his disorder. Upon the diagnosis, the court will then determine proper action in regard to treatment or confinement. It is important that the terms "sexual psychopath" and "criminally insane" not be used interchangeably.

DISCUSSION QUESTIONS

1. Why are the post-trial and prejudgment proceedings important to society?
2. Why is the twenty-one-day limit from verdict to judgment important in terms of court business? Are there satisfactory safeguards during this period?
3. Explain the function of the probation officer during these proceedings.
4. Discuss generally motions for a new trial and arrest of judgment.

5. Under what conditions may a court grant a new trial?
6. Discuss the term "mentally disordered sex offender."
7. How do sexual psychopath proceedings differ from other criminal proceedings?
8. Compare the terms "sexual psychopath" and "criminally insane."

9

judgment and sentence

The final step in post-trial proceedings is that of imposing judgment and sentence and includes the granting or denial of probation if such action is, in fact, a part of the proceedings. As previously mentioned, this final action cannot be taken until all proceedings and motions that are legally required have come to a conclusion and have been disposed of in a legally acceptable manner.

PRESENCE OF DEFENDANT

The physical presence of the defendant at his arraignment for judgment and sentence is prescribed in California Penal Code section 1193, subsections 1 and 2:

> **Subsection 1.** If the conviction be for a felony, the defendant must be personally present when judgment is pronounced against him, unless, after the exercise of reasonable diligence to procure the presence of the defendant, the Court shall find that

it will be in the interest of justice that judgment be pronounced in his absence; provided, that when any judgment imposing the death penalty has been affirmed by the appellate Court, sentence may be reimposed upon the defendant in his absence by the Court from which such appeal was taken, and in the manner following, to wit: Upon receipt by the Superior Court from which such appeal is taken of the certificate of the appellate Court affirming such judgment, the Judge of the said Superior Court shall forthwith make and cause to be entered an order pronouncing sentence against the defendant, and a warrant signed by the Judge, and attested by the clerk under the seal of the Court, must be drawn, and it must state the conviction and judgment and appoint a day upon which the judgment shall be executed, which must not be less than 60 days nor more than 90 days from the time of making such order, and that, within five days thereafter a certified copy of such order, attested by the clerk under the seal of the Court, and attached to the warrant, must, for the purpose of execution, be transmitted by registered mail to the warden of the state prison having the custody of the defendant and certified copies thereof must be transmitted by registered mail to the Governor; and provided further, that when any judgment imposing the death penalty has been affirmed and sentence has been reimposed as above provided there shall be no appeal from the order fixing the time for and directing the execution of such judgment as herein provided.

The sentence must be pronounced orally and according to Penal Code section 1200:

> **Subsection 2.** If the conviction be of a misdemeanor, judgment may be pronounced against the defendant in his absence. When the defendant appears for judgment he must be informed by the Court, or by the clerk, under its direction, of the nature of the charge against him and of his plea, and the verdict, if any thereon, and must be asked whether he has any legal cause to show why judgment should not be pronounced against him.

At this point judgment is pronounced in accordance with Penal Code section 1202. It is interesting that this section refers back to the original Code section (1191) that authorizes and defines the initial procedural rules for this portion of the trial process:

> If no sufficient cause is alleged or appears to the Court at the time fixed for pronouncing judgment, as provided in Section 1191 of this code, why judgment should not be pronounced, it must thereupon be rendered; and if not rendered or pronounced within the time so fixed or to which it is continued under the provisions of Section 1191 of this code, then the defendant shall be entitled to a new trial. If the Court shall refuse to hear a defendant's motion for a new trial or when made shall neglect to determine such motion before pronouncing judgment or the making of an order granting probation, then the defendant shall be entitled to a new trial.

It is significant to note that the very next section in procedural law outlines a social safeguard. This is in contrast to most of the preceding procedural rules, which are considered constitutional safeguards. This is, however, only the first of many such sociolegal enactments which are rightly an integral part of the administration of justice. Penal Code section 1203.01 is in reality the first step in the rehabilitation process, the legalities of which we shall discuss in detail further on in our study. The section states:

> Immediately after judgment has been pronounced, the Judge and the District Attorney, respectively, shall cause to be filed with the clerk of the Court a brief statement of their views respecting the person convicted or sentenced and the crime committed, together with such reports as the probation officer may have made relative to the prisoner. The attorney for the defendant and the law enforcement agency that investigated the case may likewise file with the clerk of the Court statements of their views respecting the defendant and the crime of which he was convicted. Forthwith after the filing of such statements and reports, the clerk of the Court shall mail a copy thereof, certified by such clerk, with postage thereon prepaid, addressed to

the Department of Corrections at the prison or other institution to which the person convicted is delivered.

INDETERMINATE SENTENCES

California's indeterminate-sentence law provides that in most cases where a defendant is sentenced to state prison, he is not sentenced for a specified length of time. The sentencing is in accordance with Penal Code section 1168:

> Every person convicted of a public offense, for which imprisonment in any reformatory or state prison is now prescribed by law shall, unless such convicted person be placed on probation, a new trial granted, or the imposing of sentence suspended, be sentenced to be imprisoned in a state prison, but the Court in imposing the sentence shall not fix the term or duration of the period of imprisonment.
>
> When a defendant has been sentenced to be imprisoned in the state prison and has been committed to the custody of the Director of Corrections, if it is deemed warranted by the diagnostic study and recommendations approved pursuant to Section 5079, the Court may recall the commitment previously ordered and release him under supervision as provided by Section 1203.

Under California law, when a prisoner receives an indeterminate sentence, it is, in effect, a sentence for the maximum term. The setting of a term at something less than the maximum by the adult authority is only tentative and may be set aside and the maximum imposed for parole violations [*In re Costello*, 262 F.2d 214 (1959)].

DEGREES OF CRIME

Penal Code section 1157 is the basic section which defines the responsibility of setting the degree of a crime before the pronouncement of judgment and sentencing. In effect, the law stipulates that the fixing of a degree is exclusively the responsibility of the jury. However, when a jury trial is waived, the court must assume this responsibility. It is considered necessary that the degree be fixed and if there is a failure on the part of the jury or court to do so, then the defendant can only be sentenced to the lower degree. In a 1945 case (*People v. Brown*, 69 Cal. App. 2d 602, 159 P.2d 686), a robbery case, the jury returned a general verdict of guilty. The court then fixed the degree as robbery in the first degree and sentenced accordingly. It was held on appeal that the court was in error, and the defendant was granted a new trial. It is, therefore, extremely important that this determination be made before the sentencing process. And it is then imperative that the following procedure be adhered to during the sentencing:

> Upon a plea of guilty, or upon conviction by the Court without a jury, of a crime distinguished or divided into degrees, the Court must, before passing sentence, determine the degree. Upon the failure of the Court to so determine, the degree of the crime of which the defendant is guilty, shall be deemed to be of the lesser degree. [C.P.C., sec. 1192]
>
> Upon a plea of guilty to an information or indictment accusing the defendant of a crime divided into degrees when consented to by the prosecuting attorney in open Court and approved by the Court, such plea may specify the degree thereof and in such event the defendant cannot be punished for a higher degree of the crime than the degree specified. [C.P.C., sec. 1192.1]
>
> Upon a plea of guilty before a committing Magistrate as provided in Section 859a of this code, to a crime divided into degrees, when consented to by the prosecuting attorney in open Court and approved by such Magistrate, such plea may specify the degree thereof and in such event, the defendant cannot be punished for a higher degree of the crime than the degree specified. [C.P.C., sec. 1192.2]
>
> Upon a plea of guilty to an information or indictment for which the jury has, on a plea of not guilty, the power to recom-

mend, the discretion of imposing, or the option to impose a certain punishment, the plea may specify the punishment to the same extent as it may be specified by the jury on a plea of not guilty. Where such plea is accepted by the prosecuting attorney in open Court and is approved by the Court, the defendant cannot be sentenced to a punishment more severe than that specified in the plea. [C.P.C., sec. 1192.3]

If the defendant's plea of guilty pursuant to Section 1192.1, 1192.2 or 1192.3 of this code be not accepted by the prosecuting attorney and approved by the Court, the plea shall be deemed withdrawn and the defendant may then enter such plea or pleas as would otherwise have been available. The plea so withdrawn may not be received in evidence in any criminal, civil or special action or proceeding of any nature, including proceedings before agencies, commissions, board and tribunals. [C.P.C., sec. 1192.4]

CONCURRENT AND CONSECUTIVE SENTENCING

In certain cases where a defendant is convicted of two or more crimes, he may, depending upon the circumstances, be sentenced either concurrently or consecutively. In a concurrent sentence, he will serve out his terms in an overlapping fashion; that is, both or all terms will be served at the same time except for the overlapping portion of the longest term. A consecutive sentencing, however, calls for one term to be served followed by the other or others until all are served in succession. The imposition of concurrent or consecutive sentences is a court determination, and the court may consider such facts as are brought out in the trial through testimony and evidence and the probation report. There is no conflict here with Penal Code section 19a, which specifies the limit of one year's confinement in the county jail, as the section particularly excludes the limitation from application to consecutive terms.

The law governing terms of imprisonment upon conviction for two or more crimes is found in Penal Code section 669 and reads as follows:

> When any person is convicted of two or more crimes, whether in the same proceeding or Court or in different proceedings or Courts, and whether by judgment rendered by the same Judge or by different Judges, the second or other subsequent judgment shall direct whether the terms of imprisonment or any of them to which he is sentenced shall run concurrently, or whether the imprisonment to which he is or has been sentenced, or at the termination of the second or subsequent term of imprisonment to which he has been sentenced, as the case may be; provided, however, if the punishment for any of said crimes is expressly prescribed to be life imprisonment, whether with or without possibility of parole, then the terms of imprisonment on the other convictions, whether prior or subsequent, shall be merged and run concurrently with such life term. In the event that the Court at the time of pronouncing the second or other judgment upon such person had no knowledge of a prior existing judgment or judgments, or having knowledge, fails to determine how the terms of imprisonment shall run in relation to each other, then, upon such failure so to determine, or upon such prior judgment or judgments being brought to the attention of the Court at any time prior to the expiration of 60 days from and after the actual commencement of imprisonment upon the second or other subsequent judgments, the Court shall, in the absence of the defendant and within 60 days of such notice, determine how the term of imprisonment upon said second or other subsequent judgment shall run with reference to the prior incompleted term or terms of imprisonment. Upon the failure of the Court so to determine how the terms of imprisonment on the second or subsequent judgment shall run, the term or imprisonment on the second or subsequent judgment shall run concurrently.

Habitual Criminal. Another point of law pertinent to this section is that of adjudging an individual to be a habitual criminal.

The habitual criminal law is authorized by Penal Code section 644 as follows:

(a) Every person convicted in this State of the crime of robbery, burglary of the first degree, burglary with explosives, rape with force or violence, arson as defined in Section 447a of this code, murder, assault with intent to commit murder, train wrecking, felonious assault with a deadly weapon, extortion, kidnapping, escape from a state prison by use of force or dangerous or deadly weapons, rape or fornication or sodomy or carnal abuse of a child under the age of 14 years, or any act punishable under Section 288 of this code, conspiracy to commit any one or more of the aforementioned felonies, who shall have been previously twice convicted upon charges separately brought and tried, and who shall have served separate terms therefor in any state prison and/or federal penal institution either in this State or elsewhere, or the crime of robbery, burglary, burglary with explosives, rape with force or violence, arson, murder, assault with intent to commit murder, grand theft, bribery of a public official, perjury, subornation of perjury, train wrecking, feloniously receiving stolen goods, felonious assault with a deadly weapon, extortion, kidnapping, mayhem, escape from a state prison, rape or fornication or sodomy or carnal abuse of a child under the age of 14 years, or any act punishable under Section 288 of this code, conspiracy to commit any one or more of the aforementioned felonies, shall be adjudged a habitual criminal and shall be punished by imprisonment in the state prison for life;

(b) Every person convicted in this State of the crime of robbery, burglary of the first degree, burglary with explosives, rape with force or violence, arson as defined in Section 447a of this code, murder, assault with intent to commit murder, train wrecking, felonious assault with a deadly weapon, extortion, kidnapping, escape from a state prison by use of force or dangerous or deadly weapons, rape or fornication or sodomy or carnal abuse of a child under the age of 14 years,' or any act punishable under

Section 288 of this code, conspiracy to commit any one or more of the aforementioned felonies, who shall have been previously three times convicted, upon charges separately brought and tried, and who shall have served separate terms therefor in any state prison and/or federal penal institution, either in this State or elsewhere, of the crime of robbery, burglary, burglary with explosives, rape with force or violence, arson, murder, assault with intent to commit murder, grand theft, bribery of a public official, perjury, subornation of perjury, train wrecking, feloniously receiving stolen goods, felonious assault with a deadly weapon, extortion, kidnapping, mayhem, escape from a state prison, rape or fornication or sodomy or carnal abuse of a child under the age of 14 years, or any act punishable under Section 288 of this code, conspiracy to commit any one or more of the aforementioned felonies, shall be adjudged an habitual criminal and shall be punished by imprisonment in the state prison for life;

(c) Provided, however, that in exceptional cases, at any time not later than 60 days after the actual commencement of imprisonment, the Court may, in its discretion, provide that the defendant is not an habitual criminal, and in such case the defendant shall not be subject to the provisions of this section or of Sections 3047 and 3048 of this code;

(d) Nothing in this section shall abrogate or affect the punishment by death in any and all crimes now or hereafter punishable by death.

An interesting aspect of this particular section is the legal strength it has in inhibiting the further actions of those who are adjudged habitual criminals. The outstanding features are shown in the three positive elements that clearly show the legislative intent of the law. (1) The words "shall be adjudged an habitual criminal" show that the court has no leeway in this matter, and, as a matter of fact, if the trial court does not adjudge the individual (or has no jurisdiction to do so), the appellate court will direct the trial court to impose the proper penalty. (2) It is also made quite clear by the words "shall be punished by imprisonment in the State prison for life" that there is only one penalty designed for sentencing a defendant so adjudged. (3) The seriousness of this section is further strengthened by Penal Code section 668, which provides that "no person charged with a public offense may be subjected before conviction, to any more restraint than is necessary for his detention to answer the charge."

THE DEATH SENTENCE

At the present time the highly controversial death penalty is still very much a part of California law. Even so, we find a great reluctance on the part of juries and courts to impose capital punishment and an even greater reluctance for the governor to allow such execution to take place. But regardless of the social and moral implications involved, the legal procedures stand fast. Authorization for the imposition of a judgment of death is found in Penal Code section 1217:

> When judgment of death is rendered, a commitment signed by the Judge, and attested by the clerk under the seal of the Court must be drawn and delivered to the sheriff. It must state the conviction and judgment, and must direct the sheriff to deliver the defendant, within 10 days from the time of judgment, to the warden of the State prison of this State designated by the State Board of Prison Directors for the execution of the death penalty, to be held pending the decision upon his appeal.

Legal procedures to be followed after imposition of the death penalty are as follows:

> The Judge of the Court at which a judgment of death is had, must, immediately after the judgment, transmit to the Governor, by mail or otherwise, a statement of the conviction and judgment, and a complete transcript of all the testimony given at the trial including any arguments made by respective counsel and a copy of the clerk's transcript. [C.P.C., sec. 1218]

The Governor may thereupon require the opinion of the Justices of the Supreme Court and of the Attorney General, or any of them, upon the statement so furnished. [C.P.C., sec. 1219]

If for any reason other than the pendency of an appeal pursuant to subdivision (b) of Section 1239 of this code a judgment of death has not been executed, and it remains in force, the Court in which the conviction was had shall, on application of the District Attorney, or may upon its own motion, make and cause to be entered an order appointing a day upon which the judgment shall be executed, which must not be less than 30 days nor more than 60 days from the time of making such order; and immediately thereafter, a certified copy of such order, attested by the clerk, under the seal of the Court, shall, for the purpose of execution, be transmitted by registered mail to the warden of the state prison having the custody of the defendant; provided, that if the defendant be at large, a warrant for his apprehension may be issued, and upon being apprehended, he shall be brought before the Court, whereupon the Court shall make an order directing the warden of the state prison to whom the sheriff is instructed to deliver the defendant to execute the judgment at a specified time, which shall not be less than 30 days nor more than 60 days from the time of making such order.

From an order fixing the time for and directing the warden of the state prison to whom the sheriff is instructed to deliver the defendant to execute the judgment at a specified time, which shall not be less than 30 days nor more than 60 days from the time of making such order.

From an order fixing the time for and directing the execution of such judgment as herein provided, there shall be no appeal. [C.P.C., sec. 1227]

Notwithstanding Section 1227, where a judgment of death has not been executed by reason of a stay or reprieve granted by the Governor, the execution shall be carried out on the day immediately after the period of the stay or reprieve without further judicial proceedings. [C.P.C., sec. 1227.5]

The actual execution of the death penalty requires another complete set of legal statutes, which are found in part 3, title III, of the California Penal Code. None of these procedures may, however, be put into effect until the automatic appeal requirements have been met. Penal Code section 1239b requires an automatic appeal from any death sentence by this statement: "When upon any plea a judgment of death is rendered, an appeal is automatically taken by the defendant without any action by him or his counsel." Once the appeal has been disposed of and if the sentence is affirmed, the following statutes govern the final procedure:

> Every male person, upon whom has been imposed the judgment of death, shall be delivered to the warden of the California state prison designated by the department for the execution of the death penalty, there to be kept until the execution of the judgment. [C.P.C. sec. 3600]

> Every female person, upon whom has been imposed the judgment of death, shall be delivered to the superintendent of the California Institution for Women, there to be held pending decision upon appeal. [C.P.C., sec. 3601]

> Upon the affirmance of her appeal, the female person sentenced to death shall thereafter be delivered to the warden of the California state prison designated by the department for the execution of the death penalty, not earlier than three days before the day upon which judgment is to be executed; provided, however, that in the event of a commutation of sentence said female prisoner shall be returned to the California Institution for Women, there to be confined pursuant to such commutation. [C.P.C., sec. 3602]

> The judgment of death shall be executed within the walls of one of the state prisons designated by the Court by which judgment is rendered. [C.P.C., sec. 3603]

> The punishment of death shall be inflicted by the administration of a lethal gas. [C.P.C., sec. 3604]

> The warden of the state prison where the execution is to take place must be present at the execution and must invite the presence of two physicians, the Attorney General of the state, and

at least 12 reputable citizens, to be selected by him; and he shall at the request of the defendant, permit such ministers of the Gospel, not exceeding two, as the defendant may name, and any persons, relatives or friends, not to exceed five, to be present at the execution, together with such peace officers as he may think expedient, to witness the execution. But no other persons than those mentioned in this section can be present at the execution, nor can any person under age be allowed to witness the same. [C.P.C., sec. 3605]

After the execution, the warden must make a return upon the death warrant to the county clerk of the Court by which the judgment was rendered, showing the time, mode, and manner in which it was executed. [C.P.C., sec. 3607]

SUMMARY

After all other proceedings, including motions, have been disposed of acceptably, the final step in post-trial proceeding is the imposition of judgment and sentence.

Generally, the judgment and sentence must be made in the presence of a convicted felon but may be pronounced in the absence of a misdemeanant.

Indeterminate sentences are given without fixed terms or durations of periods of confinement. This usually means that the maximum sentence is presumed and is shortened only at the hands of a parole board or other group assigned to evaluate the offender's ability to return to the community.

Concurrent and consecutive sentences are possible when the defendant is found guilty of two or more crimes.

The law provides special proceedings for persons who come before the court as habitual criminals involved in more serious crimes.

The ultimate imposition of sentence is the death penalty. This highly controversial form of punishment provides the student of law enforcement and corrections an opportunity to discuss the rights of man and the demands of society in its most awesome form.

DISCUSSION QUESTIONS

1. Discuss all of the sociolegal implications in the judgment and sentencing proceedings.
2. Why are statements of views regarding the defendant and his crime filed after judgment? Who files such reports?
3. What are indeterminate sentences? What philosophies are extended in indeterminate sentence laws?
4. Discuss the importance of degrees of crime in relation to the sentencing procedure.
5. Compare concurrent and consecutive sentences and discuss each as to its procedural value.
6. When does a defendant become a habitual criminal? Discuss the procedure involved.
7. Discuss the procedures involved in imposing the death penalty.
8. Discuss the controversies regarding the death penalty.

＃ 10

probation

THE BASIC LAW OF PROBATION

An important and integral part of many post-trial proceedings is the consideration of probation. The basic law governing the granting or denial of probation is found in section 1203 of the California Penal Code:

> After the conviction by plea or verdict of guilty of a public offense not amounting to a felony, in cases where discretion is conferred on the Court or any board or commission or other authority as to the extent of the punishment, the Court, upon application of the defendant or of the people or upon its own motion, may summarily deny probation, or at a time fixed may hear and determine in the presence of the defendant the matter of probation of the defendant and the conditions of such probation, if granted. If probation is not denied, and in every felony case in which the defendant is eligible for probation, before any judgment is pronounced, and whether or not an application for probation has been made, the Court must immediately refer the matter to the probation officer to investigate and to report to the Court, at a specified time, upon the circumstances surrounding the crime and concerning the defendant and his prior

record, which may be taken into consideration either in aggravation or mitigation of punishment. The probation officer must thereupon make an investigation of the circumstances surrounding the crime and of the prior record and history of the defendant, must make a written report to the Court of the facts found upon such investigation, and must accompany said report with his written recommendations, including his recommendations as to the granting or withholding of probation to the defendant and as to the conditions of probation if it shall be granted. The report and recommendations must be made available to the Court and the prosecuting and defense attorneys at least two days prior to the time fixed by the Court for the hearing and determination of such report and must be filed with the clerk of the Court as a record in the case at the time of said hearing. By written stipulation of the prosecuting attorney and the defense attorney, filed with the Court, or by oral stipulation in open Court made and entered upon the minutes of the Court, the time within which the report and recommendations must be made available and filed, under the preceding provisions of this section, may be waived. At the time or times fixed by the Court, the Court must hear and determine such application, if one has been made, or in any case the suitability of probation in the particular case, and in connection therewith must consider any report of the probation officer, and must make a statement that it has considered such report which must be filed with the clerk of the Court as a record in the case. If the Court shall determine that there are circumstances in mitigation of punishment prescribed by law, or that the ends of justice would be subserved by granting probation to the defendant, the Court shall have power in its discretion to place the defendant on probation as hereinafter provided; if probation is denied, the clerk of the Court must forthwith send a copy of the report and recommendations to the Department of Corrections at the prison or other institution to which the defendant is delivered.

In every misdemeanor case, the Court may, at its option, refer the matter to the probation officer for investigation and report or summarily deny probation or summarily grant probation.

The Legislature hereby expresses the policy of the people of the State of California to be that, except in unusual cases where the interest of justice demands a departure from the declared policy, no Judge shall grant probation to any person who shall have been convicted of robbery, burglary or arson, and who at the time of the perpetration of said crime or any of them or at the time of his arrest was himself armed with a deadly weapon (unless at the time he had a lawful right to carry the same), nor to a defendant who used or attempted to use a deadly weapon upon a human being in connection with the perpetration of the crime of which he was convicted, nor to one who in the perpetration of the crime of which he was convicted willfully inflicted great bodily injury or torture, nor to any person unless the Court shall be satisfied that he has never been previously convicted of a felony in this state nor previously convicted in any other place of a public offense which would have been a felony if committed in this state.

Except as hereafter provided in this section, probation shall not be granted to any person who shall have been convicted of burglary with explosives, rape with force or violence, murder, assault with intent to commit murder, attempt to commit murder, train wrecking, kidnapping, escape from a state prison, conspiracy to commit any one or more of the aforementioned felonies, and who at the time of the perpetration of said crime or any of them or at the time of his arrest was himself armed with a deadly weapon (unless at the time he had a lawful right to carry the same), nor to a defendant who used or attempted to use a deadly weapon upon a human being in connection with the perpetration of the crime of which he was convicted willfully inflicted great bodily injury or torture, nor to any defendant unless the Court shall be satisfied that he has not been twice previously convicted of felony in this state nor twice previously convicted in any other place or places of public offenses which would have been felonies if committed in this state; nor to any defendant convicted of the crime of burglary with explosives, rape with force or violence, murder, attempt to commit murder, assault with intent to commit murder, train wrecking, extortion, kidnapping, escape from a state prison, violation of Section 286, 288, or 288a of this code, or conspiracy to commit any one or more of the aforesaid felonies, unless the Court shall be satisfied that he has never been previously convicted of a felony in this state nor previously convicted in any other place of a public offense which would have been a felony if committed in this state; nor to any defendant unless the Court shall be satisfied that he has never been previously convicted of a felony in this state nor convicted in any other place of a public offense which would have been a felony if committed in this state and at the time of the perpetration of said previous offense or at the time of his arrest for said previous offense he was himself armed with a deadly weapon (unless at the time he had a lawful right to carry the same) or he personally used or attempted to use a deadly weapon upon a human being in connection with the perpetration of said previous offense he willfully inflicted great bodily injury or torture; nor to any public official or peace officer of the state, county, city, city and county, or other political subdivision who, in the discharge of the duties of his public office or employment, accepted or gave or offered to accept or give any bribe or embezzled public money or was guilty of extortion.

In unusual cases, otherwise subject to the preceding paragraph, in which the interests of justice would best be served thereby, the Judge may, with the concurrence of the District Attorney, grant probation.

No probationer shall be released to enter another state of the United States, unless and until his case has been referred to the California Administrator, Interstate Probation and Parole Compacts, pursuant to the Uniform Act for Out-of-state Probationer and Parolee Supervision.

In those cases in which the defendant is not eligible for probation, the Judge may in his discretion refer the matter to the probation officer for an investigation of the facts relevant to sentence. The probation officer must thereupon make an investigation of circumstances surrounding the crime and prior record and history of the defendant and make a written report to the Court of the facts found upon such investigation.

The nature of probation is clearly written into many case decisions showing that probation is not a right of the defendant but rather an act of grace and clemency on the part of the court.

The concept is also stated as follows in *People v. Johnson*, 134 Cal. App. 2d 140, 285 P.2d 74: "Granting of probation, aside from being an act of clemency extended to one who has committed a crime, is also in substance and effect a bargain made by [the] people, through legislature and Courts, with [the] malefactor."

APPLICATION FOR PROBATION

According to the probation law there are varying degrees of need for an application for probation. For instance, Penal Code section 1203 states that "in every felony case in which the defendant is eligible to probation before any judgment is pronounced and whether or not an application for probation has been made, the Court must immediately refer the matter to the probation officer to investigate and report." It is obvious that no application is even required. It is customary, however, that counsel enter such an application with an understanding that the probation investigation will be made. The application itself may be made orally or in writing; there is no legal requirement for a written application.

Penal Code section 1203 also makes it clear that an application for a probation investigation may be entered even though the defendant is not eligible for probation. "In those cases in which the defendant is not eligible for probation," the section states, "the Judge may in his discretion refer the matter to the probation officer for an investigation of the facts relative to sentence. The probation officer must thereupon make an investigation of circumstances surrounding the crime and the prior record and history of the defendant and make a written report to the Court of the facts found upon such investigation." This would, of course, stand whether or not an application was formally entered, and the results of such investigation may be utilized in the determination of sentencing. An order of probation should, however, be understood as having no effect upon judgment and as being a part of neither judgment nor sentence.

The nature of probation is somewhat dependent upon the category of the case and is spelled out in the governing law. Thus we find that the court may order summary probation in misdemeanor cases. Penal Code section 1203b stipulates that "All Courts shall have power to grant probation summary in misdemeanor cases without referring such cases to the probation officer; provided, however, that unless otherwise ordered by the Court persons granted probation summary shall report only to the Court and the probation officer shall not be responsible in any way for supervising or accounting for such persons."

As we have previously pointed out, probation may not be summarily granted in felony cases, but a presentence investigation shall be made before imposition of sentence. The resulting order granting probation may be made either before or after the sentencing, depending upon the discretion of the court.

CONDITIONS OF PROBATION

In determining the conditions of probation the court has discretionary powers. That is, it may order reasonable conditions that may tend to amend the wrongdoing and/or correct the behavior of the malefactor. The law governing the conditions of probation is found in Penal Code section 1203.1:

> The Court or Judge thereof, in the order granting probation, may suspend the imposing, or the execution of the sentence and may direct that such suspension may continue for such period of time not exceeding the maximum possible term of such sentence, except as hereinafter set forth, and upon such terms and conditions as it shall determine. The Court, or Judge thereof, in the order granting probation and as a condition thereof may imprison the defendant in the county jail for a period not exceeding the maximum time fixed by law in the instant case; provided, however, that where the maximum possible term of such sentence is five years or less, then such period of suspension of imposition or execution of sentence may, in the discre-

tion of the Court, continue for not over five years; may fine the defendant in such sum not to exceed the maximum fine provided by law in such case; or may in connection with granting probation, impose either imprisonment in county jail, or fine, or both, or neither; may provide for reparation in proper cases; and may require bonds for the faithful observance and performance of any or all of the conditions of probation. In counties or cities and counties where road camps, farms, or other public work is available the Court may place the probationer in such camp, farms, or other public work instead of in jail and Section 25359 of the Government Code shall apply to probation and the Court shall have the same power to require adult probationers to work, as prisoners confined in the county jail are required to work, at public work as therein provided; and supervisors of the several counties are hereby authorized to provide public work and to fix the scale of compensation of such adult probationers in their respective counties. In all cases of probation the Court is authorized to require as a condition of probation that the probationer go to work and earn money for the support of his dependents or to pay any fine imposed or reparation condition, to keep an account of his earnings, to report the same to the probation officer and apply such earnings as directed by the Court.

In all such cases if as a condition of probation a Judge of the Superior Court sitting by authority of law elsewhere than at the county seat requires a convicted person to serve sentence at intermittent periods such sentence may be served on the order of the Judge at the city jail nearest to the place at which the Court is sitting, and the cost of his maintenance shall be a county charge.

The Court may impose and require any or all of the above-mentioned terms of imprisonment, fine and conditions and other reasonable conditions, as it may determine are fitting and proper to the end that justice may be done, that amends may be made to society for the breach of the law, for an injury done to any person resulting from such breach and generally and specifically for the reformation and rehabilitation of the probationer, that should the probationer violate any of the terms or conditions imposed by the Court in the instant matter, it shall have authority to modify and change any and all such terms and conditions and to reimprison the probationer in the county jail within the limitations of the penalty of the public offense involved. Upon the defendant being released from the county jail under the terms of probation as originally granted or any modification subsequently made, and in all cases where confinement in a county jail has not been a condition of the grant of probation, the Court shall place the defendant or probationer in and under the charge of the probation officer of the Court, for the period or term fixed for probation; provided, however, that upon the payment of any fine imposed and the fulfillment of all conditions of probation, probation shall cease at the end of the term of probation, or sooner, in the event of modification. In counties or cities and counties in which there are facilities for taking fingerprints, such marks or identification of each probationer must be taken and a record thereof kept and preserved.

Any other provision of law to the contrary notwithstanding, all fines collected by a county probation officer in any of the Courts of this State, as a condition of the granting of probation, or as a part of the terms of probation, shall be paid into the county treasury and placed in the general fund, for the use and benefit of the county.

SUMMARY

Probation has become an important and necessary part of the post-trial proceeding. This function, performed outside the courtroom, provides a look into the defendant's character and sociopsychological potential for treatment and rehabilitation. Even before his sentence is imposed, this diagnostic process begins a plan to bring him back to society and his community.

In some cases probation can be the corrective sentencing pronounced by the judge without a detention at all. In other cases a jail term and probation may be imposed. In most cases no one found guilty of misdemeanors resulting from the crimes of robbery, burglary, and arson who was armed with a deadly weapon can be granted probation.

It is clear that probation is not a right of the defendant but rather an act of grace and clemency on the part of the court.

The nature of probation is somewhat dependent upon the category of the case and is spelled out in the governing law.

In misdemeanor cases, the court may grant summary probation without referring such cases to the probation officer.

The court has great discretionary powers in determining the conditions of probation.

DISCUSSION QUESTIONS

1. Discuss the values of probation in relation to the sentencing procedures.
2. What kind of report is made by the probation officer after a *presentence investigation?*
3. Discuss the social value of probation.
4. Why are the degrees of crimes committed important to the probation function?
5. Compare applications for probation to the laws governing the granting of probation.
6. Discuss the concept of conditions of probation.
7. What would be the effect if probation were not available?
8. Compare the probation effort with the police effort.

11

proper court presentation and testimony

THE POLICE OFFICER'S ROLE IN COURT

In a very real sense the police officer must be considered an officer of the court. He is required in most jurisdictions to accomplish certain responsibilities of the court, i.e., service of subpoenas or acting in the capacity of bailiff. He is on other occasions directed by the court to perform inspection or investigative duties under special conditions. But that duty with which we are most concerned here is the implied duty to act as a witness in any criminal case, the nature of which may require his legal testimony.

The role of the officer as he appears on the witness stand is dual. A democratic process of justice demands an objective neutrality in his testimony, while the nature of his office is oriented toward the prosecution. There are some inherent frustration factors present anytime we try to build mutually antagonistic characteristics into one man, and experience has shown us that this dual responsibility has indeed produced such frustrations in many a police officer. This is not to say that the problem is an insurmountable one. We simply wish to point out that the dangers are real and that much work must be done to produce good officer attitude toward this important duty.

Some authorities have gone so far as to suggest that two kinds of policemen are needed—one to investigate for the state and another to perform the same duty for the defendant. We feel that the dangers of a "contest investigation" in criminal matters is of far more concern than the possibility of some biased testimony. This is particularly true in light of the fact that built-in safeguards in the form of cross-examination, witness credibility, and testimony impeachment are routinely employed in all courts of law.

It seems that a far better approach to the officer's role in court would be from a strictly professional and ethical standpoint. The police officer may no longer regard his position as a job or occupation. He is confronted with a professional responsibility calling for highly developed skills. And this is as true when he is on the witness stand as it is when he is performing any other of his various duties.

The officer must continuously be aware that his professional role is that of a truth seeker. His success both in and out of court depends on his ability to objectively gather data in the form of evidence. Once all available material is collected and takes on the form of evidence, he can comfortably feel his job was well done regardless of whether or not the defendant is found guilty. His "professional sense" will indicate to him that *his* part in the administration of criminal justice has been ethically performed.

The above can only be true, however, when all aspects of the responsibility are equal, that is, when the job has been performed skillfully in every respect. The proper attitude must first be present, but also good procedures must be followed if success is to be achieved. We shall look at some of these procedural techniques in the following paragraphs.

THE IMPORTANCE OF APPEARANCE, MANNER, DEMEANOR, AND SPEECH

One of the basic beliefs of American society is that a professional man should look his part. It is expected that the physician, the attorney, or the business executive will follow style trends and serve his clientele with a "look" that instills confidence. Moreover, a basic principle of social psychology contends that a good appearance generates an acceptance of any individual that cannot be duplicated by other means. Even though appearances are likely to falsely convey a person's real personality, they are nonetheless important when personal decisions will rest on the resulting evaluations. These commonly known and practiced principles would not deserve further mention here except that they do affect the police officer on the witness stand.

The American courtroom usually reflects a sense of dignity. The judge sits high in the room garbed in traditional black gown. His role calls for this psychological advantage. He must make important decisions that affect many lives in many ways. His austere appearance and his elevated position simply emphasize his authority and strengthen the acceptance of his skill and responsibility.

The attorneys have also developed a mode of dress to fit their role. They are concerned with social acceptance by the jury and the judge. They take great pains to be well groomed and wear stylish, but slightly conservative, suits that imply good taste without extremes in either price or ultracontemporary design. The police officer must follow the attorney's example. He must be at least as well dressed as the attorneys and tend toward the conservative if he is to enjoy the same advantages as they.

In all possible instances the police officer should appear in a business suit of gray, brown, or light blue. He should avoid the darker, more formal colors so as not to appear compulsive or overdone. The suit should be clean and pressed and not loaded down with bulging pockets. Voluminous notes, reports, cigarettes and cigars, and, particularly, weapons should not be either directly visible or suggested by a protruding bulge in the clothing. A white shirt and matching tie, coordinated socks, and shined shoes will complete the proper attire for courtroom appearances.

If an officer is to appear during his tour of duty, he may well be in uniform, having had no opportunity to change. In these cases the officer should take great pains to see that the uniform is in good condition. He should also remove his equipment belt and all weapons. The uniform should be stripped of all visible working paraphernalia, such as keys and handcuffs. He should not wear a helmet or hat into the courtroom. In short, he should make himself as inconspicuous and as little awesome as possible. A good rule to follow is to try to change into civilian clothing. It is certainly preferred.

Equally important as his clothing is the officer's manner, demeanor, and speech. If he looks the part of the role he is playing, he must also behave within its conditional limits. The courtroom drama can be favorably compared to the staged productions with which we are all familiar. The basic difference is that the courtroom enactment unfolds with real people testifying to real experiences and producing real evidence. The comparison is valid in that both trial and play consist of recountings of past experiences and findings rather than original, spontaneous occurrences at the time of testimony. If we accept this concept, it then follows that the officer-witness is playing a role in which he is to communicate certain facts. These facts or truths are generally the result of his investigation and may be the most important testimony offered during the trial.

The officer's manner and demeanor on the stand may well set the tone for the weight his testimony will receive from the judge and jury. He must appear serious but not stiff, interested but not biased, calm but not overconfident. Most officers approach the stand under some nervous strain and anxiety. This is comparable to that feeling common to actors and public speakers called "stage fright." It is a phenomenon natural to our society and experienced by many persons without devastating results. It has, in fact, been said that the speaker or actor owes a little nervousness to his audience. Perhaps the policeman owes this same concern to the court and the defendant. Since all persons are different in their psychological reactiveness, there can be no formula for overcoming and controlling nervousness. We can only offer some guidelines that may help.

The officer should take some time to study his own nervous habits and identify those which he may unconsciously exhibit. His facial characteristics may take on a disturbing aspect to other people; he may pull at his ear, wring his hands, or tap his foot, or combine these or other physical actions. Once they are identified, the officer can consciously concentrate on overcoming such actions. His role demands that he sit comfortably straight, hands in lap, both feet on the floor, looking to the attorneys and jury with a calm confidence in himself and his work.

Another very important factor in effective presentation of testimony is proper use of the voice. Most testimony is given verbally, and that which is not is usually explained verbally. The officer must communicate his ideas in such a way that they are understood in context and in content. His voice should express the same essential characteristics that are expressed by his dress, manner, and demeanor. He should speak at a moderate rate, in as neutral a tone as possible, and without exhibiting emotion or nervousness. He should speak loudly enough to be heard by everyone, but never shout. He should speak to the jury and the attorneys, practicing good eye contact and emotional control.

When on the witness stand the officer should keep uppermost in his mind that his role is one of furnishing truthful information relative to the case. He is rarely expected to give lengthy, detailed, verbal reports without help from the attorneys. His role is neither to prosecute nor to defend, but to assist in the fact-finding processes of both. He will, therefore, be guided through his testimony by the attorneys, who will ask pertinent questions within the legal framework of criminal procedure. He is required to answer such questions according to his personal experiences and professional findings. The way in which he answers such questions may well determine the outcome of the case. He should answer each question deliberately and with caution. He should pause after each inquiry is made in case the other attorney wishes to lodge an objection to the question. If an objection is made, he must remain silent until the judge rules on whether or not the question is to be answered.

The nature of the adversary system in criminal procedure necessarily places upon the attorneys a burden of loyalty to a particular side of the case. This condition is reflected in the manner in which the attorney will approach the officer-witness. It is, for example, a duty of the defense counsel to do all in his power to lessen the weight and credibility of testimony for the prosecution. When tactics are employed in this direction, it becomes increasingly important that the officer not reflect personal affront or defensiveness in his demeanor or verbal control. To remain calm, confident, and unruffled is by far the best defense against this type of offense. Once an officer has gained a reputation for good behavior characteristics on the witness stand, it is not likely that he will be subjected to abuse because abuse that does not have the desired effect of upsetting the witness usually makes the defense attorney appear foolish.

PREPARATION FOR COURT

In truth the officer begins his preparation for court at the moment he begins an investigation. Long before he may even have a suspect in mind he will be taking steps to identify, gather and preserve, and document admissible evidence and information for possible courtroom use. Here, however, we shall assume that this responsibility has been met and deal with the actual preparation of this material toward the fulfillment of the court role of the testifying officer.

It is very likely that the officer will have a variety of materials that may be presented. He will undoubtedly have notes and reports with which to refresh his recall of the case. He will also likely have statements of witnesses, victims, and the accused. He may, in addition, have physical evidence and documentary reproductions of the crime scene such as photographs and sketches. Any or all such evidence may play an important part in his testimony. It becomes a necessity that he carefully study and examine all such materials and be thoroughly familiar with them before taking the stand. Much ineffective police testimony is a direct result of the officer's failure to make such a review prior to court time.

It is imperative, as well, that the officer and the prosecutor work closely in evidence preparation. The types and amounts of evidence needed become the responsibility of the prosecutor, and he will control what is to be presented. In all cases, the prosecutor should confer with his officer-witness, giving him an idea of the order of presentation and what he hopes to prove through testimony.

If physical and documentary evidence is to be presented, it should be prepared well ahead of the trial. Physical evidence should be labeled and marked in such a manner that it does not confuse the jurors but, rather, strengthens the verbal testimony that it accompanies.

Crime scene and comparative photographs should be mounted and labeled clearly so as to show the specific purpose for which they are intended. Crime scene sketches should be well drawn to scale and large enough to be an effective visual aid to testimony. Equipment to be used in presentation should be thoroughly checked just prior to being moved into the courtroom. It is becoming more and more common to use slide and motion picture projectors, audio- and videotape machines, and other such mechanical devices to more graphically portray evidence to the senses of the court. It is incumbent upon the officer to see to these details. If he does not, he cannot expect to fully realize their potential value.

PRESENTATION OF EVIDENCE

Once on the witness stand, the officer who is to present testimony and physical evidence will be largely controlled by the prosecutor. It is the prosecuting attorney's job to decide what evidence to bring out and the order in which it is to be presented. The officer, then, will follow the directions set and produce such information as it is needed. When answering questions verbally he need only adhere to the guidelines described earlier in this chapter. When presenting documentary or other kinds of physical evidence he may be required to provide a more detailed and less structured type of testimony, often with an explanatory speech. A traffic investigator, for example, may be asked to draw a diagram on a chalkboard to illustrate his findings at the scene of an accident, or a fingerprint technician may be required to produce comparative photographs of a latent and a rolled fingerprint and explain why they are considered to be positively the same print pattern. In these kinds of cases, the officer must be well prepared and ready to answer questions with sound and convincing answers.

USE OF NOTES

It is well established in procedural rules that a witness may use notes with which to refresh his memory. Obviously there will be times when one must refer to specific notations to be absolutely accurate. Because of this necessity it is well that an officer's notes be readily available and in good order. It should, however, be pointed out that once such notes are produced, they can and likely will be read by the counsel for the defense. This, too, is perfectly all right, if the notes concern this case only and include no grocery lists or girl friends' phone numbers. The obvious point here is that an entire notebook should not be produced but only those notes pertinent to the case at issue. Another point of importance is that when two officers have merged their activities into one set of notes, this fact should be documented on the notes. Also both officers should know the contents of such notes and agree on their meaning.

One final word of caution. The courtroom is no place to practice the art of bluffing. Every officer, at one time or another, will be in a position where the bluff will be a great temptation. He must not succumb to it. If he does, he is jeopardizing his entire testimony. A bluff, when called, makes the perpetrator appear foolish and incompetent. In addition, it may be legal grounds for impeachment of his testimony and will most certainly diminish its credibility and weight.

SUMMARY

The role of the police officer as a witness in court is a dual one. He is bound to act as a witness for the prosecution and must also be the pillar of objective neutrality in his testimony. The officer must constantly be aware that his professional role is that of a truth seeker.

Appearance, manner, demeanor, and speech are of the utmost importance to the police officer fulfilling his responsibility in court.

The preparation to appear as a witness begins the moment an investigation is underway and continues until the testimony is given. The officer must take every opportunity to prepare his material in the best possible way if he is to be considered professional in his approach.

Once on the witness stand the officer must be prepared to present evidence at the prosecutor's request. It is now the prosecutor who has prime responsibility, and the officer must not overstep his bounds into that realm of control.

The courtroom is no place to practice the art of bluffing. This kind of behavior can only result in disaster for the case at hand and the officer's future reliability.

DISCUSSION QUESTIONS

1. Discuss the police officer's role in court.
2. Why does the officer have a dual responsibility in court?
3. What best describes the police officer's professional role as applied to the giving of testimony?
4. In what ways do the officer's appearance, manner, demeanor, and speech affect his ability as a witness?
5. How can an officer improve his mannerisms in preparation for court?
6. Discuss the officer's responsibility in preparing for court.
7. Why must the officer and prosecutor work closely in preparing the case?
8. Once on the witness stand the officer is dependent upon the prosecutor. Why? Discuss this philosophy.
9. May an officer refer to notes on the witness stand? Why? Discuss this issue in detail.

12

laws of arrest

Of utmost importance to the police officer in the field is that set of legal procedural rules pertaining to the taking into custody of a suspected offender. These procedures are very complex in their entirety, but we shall present only those concepts needed to fullfill the practical and legal requirements of the routine arrest. It should be recognized that there are two general ways in which an arrest will be made. It may, in the first instance, be made under the authorization of a warrant issued by the court and served by a peace officer or, in the second, by a peace officer or private citizen without a warrant. We shall discuss both processes.

ARREST WITH WARRANT

Generally we may say that an arrest under the authorization of a warrant is the most desirable from the police officer's viewpoint. In these cases the preliminary investigations have necessarily established a corpus delicti and probable belief of the suspect's guilt. This is certainly a more functional framework within which to work than is the on-the-street arrest with its inherent problems of haste and ambiguity. The most beneficial factor of the arrest with warrant is that the court is already involved and has committed itself to further inquiry. California Penal Code section 813 states:

> When a complaint is filed with a magistrate charging a public offense originally triable in the superior court of the county in which he sits, if such magistrate is satisfied from the complaint that offense complained of has been committed and that there is reasonable ground to believe that the defendant has committed it, he must issue a warrant for the arrest of the defendant; provided, that when the magistrate is a judge of the justice court, he may issue such a warrant only upon the concurrence of the district attorney of the county in which he sits or the Attorney General of the State of California.

In general this is the law that authorizes the issuance of a warrant of arrest and outlines its elements. All of its parts must be complied with to make it binding:

1. It must be filed with a magistrate.
2. It must contain a charge triable in the Superior Court.
3. The magistrate must believe that the offense has been committed and that the named defendant committed it.

The Warrant. The form of the warrant as shown in California Penal Code section 813 should substantially meet the following requirements:

County of _____

The people of the State of California to any peace officer of said state:

Complaint on oath having this day been laid before me that the crime of _____ (designating it generally) has been committed and accusing _____ (naming defendant) thereof, you are therefore commanded forthwith to arrest the above named defendant and bring him before me at _____

(naming the place), or in case of my absence or inability to act, before the nearest or most accessible magistrate in this county.
Dated at _____ (place) this _____ day of _____, 19___.

Signature and full official title of magistrate

In general it can be stated that "a 'warrant' is a process issued in the name of the state directed to any sheriff, constable, marshal, or policeman commanding him to arrest and take into custody the named defendant." [*Pankewicz v. Jess*, 27 Cal. App. 340, 149 Pac. 997 (1915)] California Penal Code section 815 further defines the contents of a warrant by stipulating that the defendant's name must appear on the document if the name is known. If the name is not known, the warrant may be made out in any name. (If the name is unknown it will usually bear the fictitious name of "John Doe" if the defendant is a male or "Jane Doe" if the defendant is female.) It is further stipulated in this section that the time of issuance must be stated, as must the city and county, county, city, town, or township where it is issued. It must also be signed by the magistrate, judge, or justice issuing it along with a designation of his title of office.

Another element vital to the legality of the issuance of a warrant of arrest is the provision that the magistrate will endorse on the warrant a fixed amount of bail. This must be done in accordance with California Penal Code section 1275. (Bail will be discussed in detail further on in this chapter.)

Finally, and in accordance with California Penal Code section 816, "a warrant of arrest must be directed generally to any peace officer in the state, and may be executed by any of those officers to whom it may be delivered."

Execution of Service. Once a warrant for arrest has been issued by a magistrate, it becomes the responsibility of the peace officer to whom it has been directed to carry out its execution. It is important to realize that such a procedural order of the court requires execution whenever possible. An officer who receives a warrant, valid on its face, has the specific duty to make the prescribed arrest [*Barrier v. Alexander*, 100 Cal. App. 2d 497, 224 P.2d 436 (1950)].

In the above decision the responsibility is also linked with a protective concept toward the officer as is expressed in the following quote: "Where a warrant, valid in form and issued by a court of competent jurisdiction, is placed in hands of an officer for execution, it is his duty without delay to carry out its command, and officer will incur no liability, however disastrous may be effect of its execution upon person against whom it is issued, if process is properly executed by officer."

The words "properly executed" are echoed by a warning well stated in *Walton v. Will*, 66 Cal. App. 2d 509, 152 P.2d 639 (1944), which states in part: "It is the officer's duty promptly to execute a warrant of arrest, but officer also owes duty to public and to person about to be arrested, and if he carelessly arrests wrong person he is liable for damages caused."

It should be noted that proper methods of taking an individual into custody must be adhered to in any case if the legal and ethical requirements of this function are to be met. In the following section of this chapter we shall discuss such methods.

The law further provides for the exact application of what is to be done with the defendant after the service of a warrant of arrest is executed. This procedure is outlined in detail in section 821 of the California Penal Code:

> If the offense charged is a felony, and the arrest occurs in the county in which the warrant was issued, the officer making the arrest must take the defendant before the magistrate who issued the warrant, or some other magistrate of the same county.
>
> If the defendant is arrested in another county, the officer must, without unnecessary delay, inform the defendant in writing of his right to be taken before a magistrate in that county, note on the warrant that he has so informed defendant and, upon being required by the defendant, take him before a magis-

trate in that county, who must admit him to bail in the amount specified in the endorsement referred to in Section 815a and direct the defendant to appear before the court or magistrate by whom the warrant was issued on or before a day certain which shall in no case be more than 10 days after such admittance to bail. If bail be forthwith given, the magistrate shall take the same and endorse thereon a memorandum of the aforesaid order for the appearance of the defendant, or if the defendant so requires, he may be released on bail set on the warrant by the issuing Court, as provided in Section 1269b of this Code without an appearance before a magistrate.

If the warrant on which the defendant is arrested in another county does not have bail set thereon, or if the defendant arrested in another county does not require the arresting officer to take him before a magistrate in that county for the purpose of being admitted to bail, or if such defendant, after being admitted to bail, does not forthwith give his bail, the arresting officer shall immediately notify the law enforcement agency requesting the arrest in the county in which the warrant was issued that such defendant is in custody, and thereafter such law enforcement agency shall take custody of such defendant within five days in the county in which he was arrested and shall take such defendant before the magistrate who issued the warrant, or before some other magistrate of the same county.

It should be noted that we have thus far dealt with that warrant of arrest commonly called the "felony warrant." We shall in everyday routine be concerned also with the misdemeanor warrant, the law regarding which is stated in section 822 of the California Penal Code and is worded substantially the same as outlined above in section 821.

Another important legal reference should be made to misdemeanor warrants and is stated in section 818 of the California Penal Code:

> In any case in which, between sunset and sunrise, a peace officer serves upon a person, at his home, apartment, hotel room, or other place of permanent or temporary abode, a war-

rant of arrest for a misdemeanor offense under the Vehicle Code or under any local ordinance relating to stopping, standing, parking, or operation of a motor vehicle and where no written promise to appear has been filed and the warrant states on its face that a citation may be used in lieu of physical arrest, the peace officer may, instead of taking the person before a magistrate, prepare a notice to appear and release the person on his promise to appear, as prescribed by Sections 853.6 through 853.8 of the Penal Code. Issuance of a notice to appear and securing of a promise to appear shall be deemed a compliance with the directions of the warrant, and the peace officer issuing such notice to appear and obtaining such promise to appear shall endorse on the warrant "Section 818, Penal Code, complied with" and return the warrant to the magistrate who issued it.

Out-of-town Warrants, Teletypes, Bulletins, etc. A substantial number of the warrants that will be executed by any law enforcement agency will originate in a jurisdiction outside that of the executing officer. We have already established that this is a legal practice in that the issuing magistrate may direct the warrant to be executed by "any peace officer in the state." For our purposes we can assume that any authorized officer of a state or local police agency may legally execute such a warrant.

In cases such as this we find that the warrant may be in the actual physical possession of the outside agency or merely that valid information that such a warrant exists may be in some manner transmitted. Either will suffice as a legal cause for execution. We can be guided by the law in these matters as it appears in section 842 of the California Penal Code: "An arrest by a peace officer acting under a warrant is lawful even though the officer does not have the warrant in his possession at the time of the arrest, but if the person arrested so requests it, the warrant shall be shown to him as soon as practicable."

Further examination shows that section 850 extends the manner in which warrant information may be transmitted to the possible arresting agency. It states:

A telegraphic copy of a warrant or an abstract of a warrant may be sent by telegraph, * * * teletype, or any other electronic devices, to one or more peace officers, and such copy or abstract is as effectual in the hands of any officer, and he must proceed in the same manner under it as though he held the original warrant issued by a magistrate. An abstract of the warrant as herein referred to shall contain the following information: the charge, the court of issuance, the subject's name, address and description, the bail, the name of the issuing magistrate, whether the offense charged is a felony or misdemeanor, and if a misdemeanor, whether it has been certified for night service, and the warrant number.

We shall no doubt find that the majority of such cases will be expedited through the medium of teletype, which provides a rapid and efficient means of police communications. It should be noted, however, that the most recent amendment to the above section is the provision that the warrant may be sent by "any other electronic devices," providing an open door to even more effective means of executing these kinds of cases.

ARREST WITHOUT A WARRANT

The arrest without a warrant is generally an arrest made by a peace officer in the field or, in some cases, an arrest by a private citizen. These kinds of arrests are not made under the sanction of the warrant and therefore are governed by a different set of laws. The police officer who must arrest in this manner assumes the responsibility of his arrest and is required to justify his actions. He must then be thoroughly familiar with the legal procedures and practices concerning arrest before such an action can be at all effective.

Arrest by Peace Officers. The modern-day law regarding peace officer arrests without a warrant has become so complex that large volumes have been written concerning its implementation and implication. Here, however, we shall concern ourselves primarily with the legal procedural aspects of arrest, with little attempt at comparative evaluation.

California Penal Code sections 834 and 835 define arrest as it applies to our study:

> An arrest is taking a person into custody, in a case and in the manner authorized by law. An arrest may be made by a peace officer or by a private person.
>
> An arrest is made by an actual restraint of the person, or by submission to the custody of an officer. The person arrested may be subjected to such restraint as is reasonable for his arrest and detention.

The above two sections reflect the general law of arrest. In order to more specifically define arrests as made by peace officers we turn to California Penal Code section 836:

> A peace officer may make an arrest in obedience to a warrant, or may, pursuant to the authority granted him by the provisions of Chapter 4.5 (commencing with Section 830) of Title 3 of Part 2, without a warrant, arrest a person:
> 1. Whenever he has reasonable cause to believe that the person to be arrested has committed a public offense in his presence.
> 2. When a person arrested has committed a felony, although not in his presence.
> 3. Whenever he has reasonable cause to believe that the person to be arrested has committed a felony, whether or not a felony has in fact been committed.

Again, we find that this basic law regarding peace officer arrests is of a very general nature. We should not be caught in the all-too-common trap of believing that any wording of a legal statute may be read in its widest interpretations. This is especially true of the laws of arrest. There are in fact hundreds of case citations that act as guidelines to the officer who must make arrests under many varied and complex situations. A few such citations follow in an effort to clarify some of the more common questions that arise in many arrest situations:

> No exact formula exists for determining reasonable cause to believe the person to be arrested has committed a felony so as to justify an arrest without a warrant, and each case must be decided on the facts and circumstances presented to the arresting officers at the time they were required to act. [*People v. Ross,* 60 Cal. Rptr. 254, 429 P.2d 606 (1967)]
>
> Arrest without a warrant can only be legally made if the person arrested has committed public offense in the presence of arresting officer or if arresting officer has reasonable cause to believe that the person arrested has committed felony. [*People v. Holmes,* 47 Cal. Rptr. 246, 237 Cal. App. 2d 795 (1965)]
>
> A police officer may make an arrest when he has reasonable cause to believe the person arrested has committed a felony and in fact it is the officer's duty to do so. [*People v. Poole,* 174 Cal. App. 2d 57, 344 P.2d 30 (1959)]
>
> California permits arrest without a warrant if an officer has probable cause to believe that the person arrested has committed a felony. [*Ferganchick v. U.S.,* 374 F.2d 559, 87 Sup. Ct. 2085, 387 U.S. 947, 18 L. Ed. 2d 1337 (1967)]
>
> No warrant is required for arrest by California officers of one whose arrest is made during his violation of law in the presence of arresting officers. [*Morales v. U.S.,* 344 F.2d 846, *appeal after remand,* 373 F.2d 527 (1965)]
>
> "Presence" in this section providing that peace officer may arrest person without a warrant whenever officer has reasonable cause to believe that person to be arrested has committed a public offense in his "presence" of officer is liberally construed and neither physical proximity nor sight is essential. [*In re McDonald,* 58 Cal. Rptr. 29 (1967)]

The above are only a few of the more recent guidelines handed down by the various courts, but they are indicative of the current trend. The laws of arrest and those laws which are closely associated with arrest procedures should be carefully watched because they can and do change to conform with each development toward higher legal sophistication.

Two other procedural statutes which should be noted in this area are found in sections 840 and 841 of the California Penal Code:

> If the offense charged is a felony, the arrest may be made on any day, and at any time of the day or night. If it is a misdemeanor, the arrest cannot be made at night, unless upon the direction of the magistrate, indorsed upon the warrant, except when the offense is committed in the presence of the arresting officer.
>
> The person making the arrest must inform the person to be arrested of the intention to arrest him, of the cause of the arrest, and the authority to make it, except when the person making the arrest has reasonable cause to believe that the person to be arrested is actually engaged in the commission of or an attempt to commit an offense, or the person to be arrested is pursued immediately after its commission, or after an escape.
>
> The person making the arrest must, on request of the person he is arresting, inform the latter of the offense for which he is being arrested.

In reference to the latter of the above statutes, it is well to include the information regarding the arrest as a routine act in every case. This can and should be done at the same time the accused is being advised of his constitutional rights.

This once-over-lightly approach to the law of arrest is certainly inadequate to properly inform the field police officer in all aspects of this important responsibility. It does, however, place the procedural concepts in their proper perspective in terms of the administration of criminal justice. We should emphasize that in the absence of a properly executed arrest, the remaining judicial process will be greatly endangered, or in some cases rendered impossible.

Arrest by Private Citizens. In a legal system such as ours which relies heavily on citizen support and participation, it is not surprising that a citizen's arrest procedure is a well-accepted doctrine of law. We find such authorization in California Penal Code section 837:

> **Arrests by Private Persons.** A private person may arrest another:
> 1. For a public offense committed or attempted in his presence.
> 2. When the person arrested has committed a felony, although not in his presence.
> 3. When a felony has been in fact committed, and he has reasonable cause for believing the person arrested to have committed it.

In comparison with peace officer powers of arrest we find only one major difference in the general structure of the law, namely the added authority of the peace officer to arrest a suspected felon on reasonable cause, even though it is not at the time known if a felony has in fact been committed. The assumption is that the professional law enforcement officer can make such an arrest on solid investigatory fact and to a higher degree of competency than can the average citizen.

There are few cases of citizen arrests where a police officer does not play a significant role in the eventual judicial process. His and the citizen's responsibility in such an arrest are spelled out in California Penal Code section 847:

> A private person who has arrested another for the commission of a public offense must, without unnecessary delay, take the person arrested before a magistrate, or deliver him to a peace officer. There shall be no civil liability on the part of and no cause of action shall arise against any peace officer, acting within the scope of his authority, for false arrest or false imprisonment arising out of any arrest when:
> (a) Such arrest was lawful or when such peace officer, at the

time of such arrest had reasonable cause to believe such arrest was lawful; or
(b) When such arrest was made pursuant to a charge made, upon reasonable cause, of the commission of a felony by the person to be arrested; or
(c) When such arrest was made pursuant to the requirements of Penal Code Sections 142, 838 or 839.

In an attorney general's opinion we find that "when a person is arrested by a peace officer or private person without a warrant, the arresting officer, private person, or peace officer to whom the arrested person is delivered, is required to take such arrested person before the nearest and most accessible magistrate without unnecessary delay. It is further the opinion of the Attorney General that a peace officer, under authority of Section 849, may issue a citation to a person arrested by a private person for the commission of a misdemeanor when such person has been placed in the custody of the officer by the arresting party.

"Arresting officer or peace officer, who receives custody of a prisoner from private person, has the primary responsibility for transporting such arrested person from the county or city jail to the magistrate's court on a first appearance, but once the arresting process has been completed, and the prisoner has been produced in court, and a complaint has been laid before the magistrate, the functions of the arresting officer are at an end."

In order to see that the law regarding citizen's arrest is not to be considered lightly, we need but refer to California Penal Code section 142, which states: "Every sheriff, coroner, keeper of a jail, constable, or other peace officer, who willfully refuses to receive or arrest any person charged with a criminal offense, is punishable by a fine not exceeding five thousand dollars, or by imprisonment in the state prison not exceeding five years or in a county jail not exceeding one year, or by both such fine and imprisonment."

The Doctrine of Reasonable Cause. The terms "reasonable cause" and "probable cause" appear time and again in reference to arrests by both officers and private parties. As with most other facets of this complex set of statutory rules we shall deal rather generally with these terms. Although they appear separately as well as in a conjunctive form in many statutes and case decisions, they have for all practical purposes the same legal meaning and may correctly be used interchangeably. It is of utmost importance that this meaning be thoroughly understood by every police officer. The following selected information from recent court decisions generally reflects the present attitude toward these terms:

> Reasonable or probable cause sufficient to authorize an arrest without a warrant exists when the facts and circumstances within the knowledge of the officers at the moment of the arrest are sufficient to warrant a prudent man in believing that the defendant has committed an offense. [*People v. Talley*, 56 Cal. Rptr. 492, 423 P. 2d 564, 65 Cal. 2d 830 (1967)]
>
> "Reasonable cause" to believe the person to be arrested has committed a felony so as to authorize arrest without a warrant is defined as that state of facts which would lead a man of ordinary care and prudence to believe and conscientiously entertain an honest and strong suspicion that the person is guilty of a crime. [*People v. Ross*, 60 Cal. Rptr. 254, 429 P.2d 606 (1967)]
>
> Test of reasonable cause for arrest is whether there is more evidence for than against, so that a man of ordinary care and prudence, knowing what arresting officer knows, would be led to believe or conscientiously entertain strong suspicion of doubt, although reserving some possibility for doubt. [*People v. Murietta*, 60 Cal. Rptr. 56 (1967)]
>
> Probable cause for an arrest is shown if a man of ordinary caution and prudence would be led to believe or conscientiously entertain a strong suspicion of guilt of the accused. [*People v. Thomas*, 59 Cal. Rptr. 22 (1967)]
>
> Probable cause for arrest without a warrant is not limited to evidence that would be admissible at trial on issue of guilt; the test is whether the facts as they appear to the officer at the time of arrest were such that a reasonable man would conclude that

the arrested person should be held to answer. [*People v. Tillman*, 47 Cal. Rptr. 614, 238 Cal. App. 2d 134 (1965)]

As can readily be seen, the legal meanings of "reasonable" and "probable" are based on what would be ordinary and prudent to the "average" man. Under these conditions there can be no set of rigid rules. If the officer understands the general tenor of the terms, he must accept that each case will be weighed on its own merits.

DUTIES DURING AND AFTER ARREST

During and immediately after the execution of an arrest there are certain specific and implied duties that must concern the arresting officer. We have already mentioned the importance of advising the defendant of the intention to arrest, the cause of the arrest, and the authority under which the arrest is being made. Even though it may seem a redundant and unnecessary exchange of words, the officer will find it much to his ultimate advantage if he carefully explains in detail the mechanics of the arrest. The arrest is becoming an increasingly critical point of focus in the criminal justice picture and must not be taken lightly, regardless of its routineness to either the officer or the defendant.

A question often raised in the process of arrest is that which refers to the physical and forceful breaking into of a home or establishment in order to effect an arrest. The law stated in California Penal Code section 844 is as follows:

> To make an arrest, a private person, if the offense be a felony, and in all cases a peace officer, may break open the door or window of the house in which the person to be arrested is, or in which they have reasonable grounds for believing him to be, after having demanded admittance and explained the purpose for which admittance is desired.

As in most cases of this nature we find that court decisions have been rendered which provide further guidelines to the officer. In making such field decisions he can once again turn to the doctrine of "reasonable cause":

> "Reasonable grounds," within this section authorizing officer to make forcible entry to arrest, is substantial equivalent of terms (reasonable cause and probable cause) in constitutional and statutory provisions pertaining to issuance of search warrant, arrest without warrant, a commitment or indictment. [*People v. Pease*, 51 Cal. Rptr. 448, 242 Cal. App. 2d 442 (1966)]

Another decision throws further light on the subject:

> This section, forbidding peace officer from breaking into houses to arrest felons unless he has first demanded admittance and explained purpose for which admittance is desired, does not require literal compliance would increase officer's peril or frustrate arrest. [*People v. Carrillo*, 50 Cal. Rptr. 185, 412 P.2d 377 (1966)]

The key to performing successful arrests under these conditions is in the officer's reasonable conduct, acting on solid information and suspicion. Without going deeply into the question of physical force and resistance to arrest, we should at least look at three major statutes dealing with this subject. California Penal Code section 835a outlines the peace officer's duties as follows:

> Any peace officer who has reasonable cause to believe that the person to be arrested has committed a public offense may use reasonable force to effect the arrest, to prevent escape, or to overcome resistance.
> A peace officer who makes or attempts to make an arrest need not retreat or desist from his efforts by reason of the resistance or threaten the resistance of the person being arrested; nor shall such officer be deemed an aggressor or lose his right to self defense by the use of reasonable force to effect the arrest or to prevent escape or to overcome resistance.

Again we find the term "reasonable," the meaning of which must comply with its legal spirit as previously described. In this rather delicate area of law of arrest we find that the peace officer is not alone in legal requirement but that the arrestee must also comply with his own responsibility to the law. Penal Code section 834 states: "If a person has knowledge, or by the exercise of reasonable care, should have knowledge, that he is being arrested by a peace officer, it is the duty of such person to refrain from using force or any weapon to resist such arrest."

It is further stated in *People v. Burns*, 18 Cal. Rptr. 921, 198 Cal. App. 2d Supp. 839 (1961), that it "is not unwarranted invasion of constitutional and fundamental rights" to require a person being arrested to comply with such a responsibility. And *People v. Baca*, 55 Cal. Rptr. 681, 247 Adv. Cal. App. 487 (1966) adds: "A citizen subjected to attempted arrest by one known to be a police officer must submit quietly and settle his rights at the station and in the courts, not on the street corner."

Finally we should examine California Penal Code section 843, which provides for the use of force in effecting an arrest by warrant: "When the arrest is being made by an officer under the authority of a warrant, after information of the intention to make the arrest, if the person to be arrested either flees or forcibly resists, the officer may use all necessary means to effect the arrest."

Defendant's Right to Counsel. Of ever-increasing importance to the arrest procedure is the officer's responsibility to guarantee to the arrested his constitutional rights. This is a relatively new responsibility of the peace officer and has required a rather drastic change in his traditional role. As well as playing the part of an enforcer of the law, he must also be prepared to adequately protect the citizen from a deprivation of his basic rights. One of these rights is to be represented by an attorney.

There are some legal implications in these cases that demand constant attention. There is no need to provide the defendant with counsel immediately upon arrest, but he must be advised that he is entitled to an attorney and that if he is unable to obtain private counsel, he will be provided with one free of charge. Not only must he be advised of this, he must understand it. The officer must be prepared to show that such requirements have been met.

It goes without saying that under no conditions may the defendant be denied the right to seek, obtain, and talk to an attorney.

Defendant's Right to Remain Silent. In conjunction with and closely associated with his right to legal counsel, the defendant has also a definite right to remain silent in the face of his accusers. This guaranteed constitutional right also requires an admonition or warning on the part of arresting officers. Such a warning should be made verbally at the time of arrest and in writing at the time of booking. The important element here is that the defendant be made aware that he does not have to talk to anyone unless he wishes to do so and that anything he does say may be used against him in a court of law. Once again, his awareness must be coupled with understanding.

The Legal Admonishment. In an effort to standardize the legal requirements of the rights both to counsel and to silence, a warning or admonishment form has been devised and is being widely used. Such a form is necessary because of the precision on wording and understanding that is required by the courts. The face of the admonishment should substantially contain the four following phases:

1. You have the right to remain silent.
2. Anything you say can and will be used against you in a court of law.
3. You have the right to talk to a lawyer and have him present with you while you are being questioned.
4. If you cannot afford to hire a lawyer, one will be appointed to represent you before any questioning, if you wish one.

These requirements are in no way meant to suppress the arrested person who wishes to talk to the investigators regarding the case. In order to protect the evidentiary value of the case, however, the arresting officers or follow-up investigators must obtain a waiver of his rights by the arrested. This can be accomplished by securing an affirmative reply, preferably in writing, to two questions, directly following the reading of the above warning. These questions should be stated as follows:

1. Do you understand each of these rights I have explained to you?
2. Having these rights in mind, do you wish to talk to us now?

Having complied with this requirement, the investigation may progress as the case warrants.

Confessions. Since confessions are often closely associated with the initial arrest, we should say a brief word here concerning their relationship to the administration of justice.

First, confessions and admissions are not ruled out by the constitutional right to remain silent and may properly be obtained as part of the arrest procedure. It is, however, imperative that the above legal admonishment be first given.

Second, it must be kept in mind that the confession must be given freely and voluntarily. The officer must always be able to produce proof that it was so given or realize that it will not be admissible in a court of law.

Evidence. We do not wish to go into a lengthy discourse on the rules of evidence, which is a complete study in itself. We do wish, however, to point out that the gathering of evidence may well be done at or may be incidental to a lawful arrest. The admissibility of that evidence may well depend upon the degree of adherence to the arrest procedures outlined above. The successful police officer is the one who is willing in all cases to keep well within the meaning and spirit of the law and to guard the individual rights of each citizen.

EXTRADITION

"Extradition" is the act of a state in surrendering a person within its jurisdiction to another state that alleges that the person has committed a crime or has been convicted of a crime in its (the demanding state's) jurisdiction.

Extradition is provided for in the United States Constitution, Article IV, section 2: "A person charged in any state with treason, felony, or other crime, who shall flee from justice, and be found in another state, shall on demand of the executive authority of the state from which he fled, be delivered up to be removed to the state having jurisdiction of the crime."

In California, Penal Code section 1548.1 provides: "It is the duty of the Governor of this State to have arrested and delivered up to the executive authority of any other State any person charged in that State with treason, felony, or other crime, who has fled from justice and is found in this State."

The procedures for extradition have been somewhat standardized by the adoption of the Uniform Criminal Extradition Act. The procedures follow.

Arrest with a Warrant. In accordance with California Penal Code section 1548:

1. A demand in writing must be made to the state where the accused is located, alleging that the accused was present in the demanding state at the time of commission of the alleged crime and that thereafter the person fled from that demanding state.
2. A copy of the indictment, information, or affidavit made before a magistrate in the demanding state, together with a copy of the warrant, a copy of the judgment or conviction or sentence imposed, and a statement that the person has escaped or

violated the terms of probation, parole, or bail must accompany the demand.
3. Once the demand has been made, the governor may call for an investigation of the demand by the attorney general or district attorney to ascertain the facts and whether the person should be surrendered to the demanding state.
4. If the investigation supports the demand, then the governor signs a warrant of arrest, which is directed to any peace officer or other person entrusted with the execution thereof.
5. After the arrest, the person must be taken before a magistrate, who informs him of the demand, the crime with which he is charged, and his right to legal counsel. The arrest may be challenged by a writ of habeas corpus. If the arrest is valid, then the person is remanded to the demanding state.

A warrant for the arrest of an accused may also be issued by a magistrate if the charge is made by verified complaint or on an affidavit that a crime was committed, or if the accused was convicted or escaped from bail, probation, or parole and is believed to be in this state.

Arrest without a Warrant. Extradition proceedings may also be instituted by the arrest of a person by a peace officer *without a warrant* upon reasonable information that the accused stands charged in the courts of another state with a crime punishable by death or imprisonment for a term exceeding one year. The procedure for such an arrest without a warrant is as follows:

1. Immediately upon the arrest, the magistrate must notify the district attorney, who must in turn give notice to the executive authority, the prosecuting attorney, or presiding judge of the jurisdiction for the committed offense in order that he may make a demand for the person.
2. The magistrate conducts a hearing to determine if the person was arrested properly and is wanted in another jurisdiction.
3. If such a determination is made, then the magistrate must

commit him to jail, for a period not to exceed thirty days, in order to allow an arrest under a governor's warrant.
4. If the accused is not arrested under a governor's warrant within thirty days, then the magistrate may recommit him for a further period of sixty days; in which event, the accused may be allowed to bail.

Waiver of Extradition. All of the above procedures may be waived by the accused if he subscribes in the presence of a magistrate to a written statement that he consents to return to the demanding state. This waiver is then filed with the governor, and the person is delivered to the representative of the demanding state (C.P.C., sec. 1555.1).

Extradition to California from Another State. If a person from California has been charged with a crime in California and he is in another state, the procedure for initiating extradition from the other state is as follows:

1. The district attorney files a written application stating the name, crime, approximate time, place, and circumstances, and the state in which he is believed to be.
2. The application is then forwarded to the state where the accused is located.

THE RIGHT TO BAIL

"Bail" is a procedure whereby a person who has been arrested may be released from custody after posting or depositing a sum of money or a bond to ensure his presence in court for further proceedings. Bail may be in the form of cash or a bond; in either form, however, it acts as security that the accused will be present for court proceedings.

Upon Arrest. After a person has been arrested and taken to the jail for processing, fingerprinting, etc., he may be released on bail. The sum of money necessary for his release or the amount of the bond is commonly referred to as the amount of bail. The officer in charge of the jail has the authority to approve and accept the payment or bond. A schedule setting forth the amount of bail for various misdemeanor offenses must be available at the jail.

It is the duty of the Municipal and Justice Court judges in each county to prepare and adopt, by a majority vote, such a schedule of bail for misdemeanor offenses. It shall contain a list of such offenses and the amounts of bail applicable thereto determined by the judges to be appropriate, and, if it does not list all misdemeanor offenses specifically, it shall contain a general clause providing for a designated amount of bail as the judges of the county determine to be appropriate for all misdemeanor offenses not specifically listed in the schedule. The schedule of bail may be revised from time to time by the judges of the county, and the senior judge at each county seat shall call not more than two nor less than one meeting each year of all Municipal and Justice Court judges in the county for the purpose of establishing or revising a countywide uniform bail schedule. A copy of the schedule shall be sent to the officer in charge of the county jail and to the officer in charge of each city jail within the county.

Upon posting such bail the defendant or arrested person shall be discharged from custody as to the offense on which the bail is posted. All money and surety bonds so deposited with such officer shall be transmitted immediately to the judge or clerk of the court by which the order was made or warrant issued or bail schedule fixed.

If a defendant or arrested person so released fails to appear at the time and in the court so ordered upon his release from custody, the court before which he was ordered to appear may forfeit the cash bail or surety bond, with or without issuing a warrant, and if the bail is a surety bond, the surety company is obligated as provided by section 1306 of the Penal Code, subject to the right of the court to set aside the forfeiture as provided by law (C.P.C., sec. 1269b).

A person who is arrested on a warrant may be released on bail for the amount of the bail that has been endorsed upon the warrant.

The magistrate in fixing the amount of bail must take into consideration the seriousness of the offense charged and the probability of the accused's appearance at further court proceedings. It must be emphasized that bail may not be excessive nor with the purpose of punishing the accused.

After Preliminary Examination. Once the accused has been held to answer after the preliminary examination, the question of being released on bail, ending the trial, arises. The magistrate may release the accused on bail upon the same considerations set forth above. The situation has changed somewhat, however, in that at this point there has been a finding of "probable cause" that the accused committed the offense. But in the majority of cases the chances are that if the accused has already been admitted to bail prior to the preliminary hearing, the magistrate will again admit him to bail.

It should be noted that there are certain requisites for bail. Penal Code section 1279 states:

> The qualifications of bail are as follows:
> 1. Each of them must be a resident, householder, or freeholder within the state; but the court or magistrate may refuse to accept any person as bail who is not a resident of the county where bail is offered;
> 2. They must each be worth the amount specified in the undertaking, exclusive of property exempt from execution, except that if any of the sureties is not worth the amount specified in the undertaking, exclusive of property exempt from execution, but owns any equity in real property, a hearing must be held before the magistrate to determine

the value of such equity. Witnesses may be called and examined at such hearing and if the magistrate is satisfied that the value of the equity is equal to twice the amount of the bond, such surety is justified. In any case, the court or magistrate, on taking bail, may allow more than two sureties to justify severally in amounts less than that expressed in the undertaking, if the whole justification be equivalent to that of sufficient bail.

Nonbailable Offenses. Bail is a matter of right except in cases where the offense is punishable by death and the presumption of guilt or evidence thereof great. The actual "right to bail," however, is limited to the magistrate's discretion where the accused may be dangerous to himself or to the community. The magistrate may also take into consideration the status of the accused in the community and the risk involved that the accused may leave the jurisdiction. The discretion of the magistrate is usually upheld except in instances where it is clearly shown that the amount of bail is excessive for the offense.

Bail may either be increased or decreased upon a showing of good cause; for example, when an accused has committed a minor offense and the bail has been set too high for no apparent reason. The bail may be reduced upon a showing that the accused is not likely to leave the jurisdiction and is a good risk to return for further court proceedings. Likewise, when the accused is out on bail for one offense and, prior to his court appearance, he is arrested on a similar charge, the bail will either be revoked and the accused remanded to custody or the bail will be increased.

Bail Proceedings. Once the accused has appeared in court at the trial, the bail will be exonerated, that is, it has no further purpose, and the money which has been deposited will be returned or the bond which has been deposited will be released.

Dismissal. When the charge has been dismissed, the bail will be exonerated.

Conviction. Upon conviction, the bail will be returned or exonerated.

Arrest by Surety. The person who deposited the funds for the amount of bail may at any time before the trial arrest the accused and take him to the officer in whose custody he was originally. For example, the bail bondsman may obtain information that the accused is going to leave the jurisdiction and arrest him in order to ensure his presence in court.

Forfeiture. If the accused fails to appear at any time designated by the court for further proceedings, the court, in addition to issuing a bench warrant for his arrest, may also order a bail forfeiture; i.e., the money or bond that has been posted must be given up to the court and after 180 days paid over to the county treasurer.

Release on Own Recognizance. A relatively recent innovation for the insurance of obtaining the defendant's appearance in court proceedings has been the release on a person's own recognizance; i.e., the court will allow a person free from custody merely upon the person's reputation and promise to appear. This type of release from custody is not a matter of right and is purely discretionary with the magistrate. The powers granted to a court or magistrate by this article are purely discretionary and permissive (C.P.C., sec. 1318.2).

In order to be released on his own recognizance, the accused must, in accordance with Penal Code section 1318.4, sign an agreement in writing whereby he agrees that:

1. He will appear at all times and places as ordered by the court or magistrate releasing him and as ordered by any court in which, or any magistrate before whom, the charge is subsequently pending.

2. If he fails to so appear and is apprehended outside the State of California, he waives extradition.
3. Any court or magistrate of competent jurisdiction may revoke the order of release and either return him to custody or require that he give bail or other assurance of his appearance as elsewhere provided by this chapter.

SUMMARY

The legal procedural rules relating to the taking of a suspected offender into custody are of utmost importance to the police officer in his daily routine.

Arrests may be made under the sanction of a warrant issued by a competent court or according to a set of rules which must be applied to the individual case.

Arrests may be made by a police officer acting in his official capacity or by a private citizen. The rules governing such arrests are spelled out in law and apply differently to the two individuals.

The doctrine of reasonable and probable cause is important to the procedure of arrest and must be adhered to in all cases.

After an arrest is made, the officer has the direct responsibility to safeguard the rights of the arrested. These rights must be clearly communicated to the defendant, and the officer must be prepared to show that such requirements have been met.

An arrest made through the process of extradition has a different set of procedural rules to follow.

The process of release may also be considered in the area of arrest. The normal channels of temporary release are through bail or release on the defendant's own recognizance.

DISCUSSION QUESTIONS

1. Discuss the procedure of making an arrest through the use of a warrant.

2. Discuss the procedure of making an arrest without a warrant.
3. Compare the two ways in which arrests may be executed and discuss their advantages and disadvantages.
4. Compare the citizen's-arrest process in relation to arrest by peace officers.
5. Discuss "reasonable cause" relative to the making of an arrest.
6. What duties must be performed by an officer during an arrest?
7. What duties must be performed by an officer directly following an arrest?
8. Discuss in detail the legal admonishment.
9. Discuss extradition as it applies to arrest.
10. What is the right to bail? What are its implications?

13

writs, motions, and appeals

WRIT OF CORAM NOBIS

The "writ of coram nobis" is a procedure whereby a party petitions the court that rendered a judgment adverse to him to review a mistake of fact at the trial. There is no statutory provision for said writ, but rather it is a procedure that has evolved through usage in the criminal courts.

The writ is not used to any great extent because of the availability of other motions to attack errors at the trial, for example, writ of habeas corpus, motion for new trial, the filing of an appeal. Its most common use is to set aside a plea of guilty on the basis that fraud, duress, coercion, or a mistake existed that induced the guilty plea.

The courts require a definite showing of diligence on the part of the defendant before they will grant the motion. His petition must show that the true facts were not known to him at the time and that he could not, in the exercise of due diligence, discover said facts.

The writ is applied for in a petition to the court that rendered the judgment. It must be under oath, and the defendant has the burden of proof to establish the grounds for the writ.

MOTION TO SET ASIDE JUDGMENT

This motion is a procedure whereby the court is requested to set aside the judgment because of its lack of validity. An example would be a judgment rendered against a defendant convicted of a crime beyond the statute of limitations. The motion is similar to a writ of coram nobis in that it seeks to set aside a judgment that has been based upon some mistake of fact or rendered upon the defendant's being induced by fraud or coercion to enter a plea of guilty.

The motion will also be denied, as in coram nobis, where its basis is better handled by an appeal, a motion for a new trial, or a writ of habeas corpus.

The procedure for filing a motion is found in Penal Code section 1201.5.

Motions Subsequent to Judgment. Any motions subsequent to judgment must be made only upon written notice served upon the prosecution at least three days prior to the date of the hearing. No affidavit or other writing shall be presented or considered in support thereof unless a copy has also been duly served upon the prosecution at least three days prior to the hearing. Any appeal from an order entered upon a motion made other than as provided here must be dismissed by the court.

MOTION FOR NEW TRIAL

A motion for a new trial is a motion for a reexamination of the issue in the same court before another court or jury.

Effect of Granting New Trials. The granting of a new trial places the parties in the same position as if no trial had been held. All the testimony must be produced anew, and the former verdict or finding cannot be used or referred to, either in evidence or in argument, or be pleaded in bar of any conviction which might have been had under the accusatory pleading (C.P.C., sec. 1180).

The grounds for a motion for a new trial are strictly statutory, and unless they are found within Penal Code section 1181, the motion will be denied. The grounds are as follows:

1. Where the defendant has been absent from the trial without any legal basis therefor
2. Where outside evidence has been received by the jury
3. Where there has been misconduct on the part of the jury, or its members have been improperly separated
4. Where the jury decided the verdict by lot or other unfair means
5. Where there have been improper instructions by the court or improper conduct by the district attorney
6. Upon error of law or a verdict rendered contrary to law
7. Upon newly discovered evidence

Procedure. The motion for a new trial must be made before judgment and is made upon an application by the defendant setting forth the basis therefor.

DEMURRER

A "demurrer" is a pleading which raises an *issue of law* as to the sufficiency of the accusatory pleading. It lies only for defects appearing on the face of the accusatory pleading.*

A demurrer generally is used when the accusatory pleading

---

* B. E. Witkin, *California Criminal Procedure*, Bender Moss Company, San Francisco, 1963, p. 220.

does not state facts sufficient to constitute a public offense, when there is no jurisdiction for the court in which the action was filed, or when pleadings clearly indicate that the statute of limitations has barred prosecution for the particular offense. An example will illustrate. The statute of limitations on a misdemeanor is one year from the commission of a crime. The accusatory pleading, which was filed in the case in point on January 10, 1967, states that the accused committed petty theft on January 5, 1966. A demurrer will be to attach the proceedings because it raises the issue of law appearing on the face of the accusatory pleading. In accordance with Penal Code section 1004, the defendant may demur to the accusatory pleading at any time prior to the entry of a plea when it appears upon the face thereof:

1. If an indictment, that the grand jury by which it was found had no legal authority to inquire into the offense charged or, if an information or complaint, that the court has no jurisdiction of the offense charged therein
2. That it does not substantially conform to the provisions of sections 950 and 952, and also section 951 in the case of an indictment or information
3. That more than one offense is charged, except as provided in section 1954
4. That the facts stated do not constitute a public offense
5. That it contains matter which, if true, would constitute a legal justification or excuse of the offense charged, or other legal bar to the prosecution

The demurrer must be in writing, signed either by the defendant or his counsel, and filed. It must clearly specify the grounds of objection to the accusatory pleading, or it must be disregarded (C.P.C., sec. 1005).

Once the demurrer is filed, a hearing is held to hear the objections to the accusatory pleading. Upon the demurrer's being filed, the argument upon the objections presented thereby must be heard immediately, unless for exceptional cause the court grants a continuance. Such continuance shall be for no longer time than the ends of justice require, and the court shall enter in its minutes the facts requiring it (C.P.C., sec. 1006).

If the demurrer is sustained, the action is dismissed against the defendant. If the demurrer is sustained with leave to amend, the amendment must be filed within the time specified. In the event the demurrer is overruled, the defendant, "must plead forthwith unless the court extends the time." (C.P.C., sec. 1007)

APPEALS BY THE DEFENDANT

The defendant in a criminal trial has a constitutional right to appeal his conviction for any specific errors that occurred at the trial or on the grounds that the evidence supporting the judgment was not sufficient. An appeal does not lie merely because the judge or jury does not agree with the defendant. Some error must be shown in the proceedings. For example, improper evidence was admitted at the trial, an erroneous instruction was given to the jury, improper argument was made to the jury, or other misconduct occurred at the trial.

THE APPELLATE COURTS

The Supreme Court. This court handles all automatic appeals where there has been a judgment of death. Any appeals from the District Court of Appeals are brought before the Supreme Court (California Constitution, art. VI, sec. 11).

District Court of Appeal. This court handles all appeals in felony cases with the exception of automatic appeal in a death case.

Superior Court. All appeals from misdemeanor cases are handled by the Superior Court. This would include any cases in either the Municipal or Justice Courts.

PROCEDURE

Appeals from Inferior Courts. The proceeding in appeals from any criminal conviction in an inferior court is strictly procedural and must be complied with in order to perfect the appeal. A notice of intent to appeal must be pleaded with the clerk or magistrate within ten days of the judgment. The defendant sets forth his grounds for appeal in a statement that must be pleaded within five days of the filing of the notice of appeal. The defendant may petition the court for extension of time within which to file a statement. The statement of grounds for the appeal must also be served upon the prosecuting attorney in order to allow him time to rebut the basis of appeal.

A hearing is held and arguments presented to support and rebut the appeal. The court may require briefs on the law to be submitted before rendering a decision on the appeal.

Appeals from Superior Courts. A written notice of appeal must be filed within ten days of the "rendition of the judgment," with the exception of a death case, where the appeal is automatically pleaded.

In felony cases, the defendant is entitled to a free transcript of the proceedings in the matter for which he had been convicted.

Formal briefs are specifically required in the appeal, and the failure to file them constitutes a ground for dismissal of the appeal.

Oral argument is also held on the basis of the appeal and the reasons for denying said appeal.

Appeals by the People. The people's, or prosecution's, right to appeal, is strictly limited by Penal Code section 1238. The basis of appeal may be only:

1. From an order setting aside the indictment information or complaint;
2. From a judgment for the defendant on a demurrer to the indictment, accusation, or information;
3. From an order granting a new trial;
4. From an order arresting judgment;
5. From an order made after judgment, affecting the substantial rights of people;
6. From an order modifying the verdict or finding by reducing the degree of the offense or the punishment imposed;
7. From an order dismissing a case prior to trial made upon motion of the court pursuant to Section 1385 whenever such order is based upon an order granting defendant's motion to return or suppress property or evidence made at a special hearing as provided in this code;
8. From an order or judgment dismissing or otherwise terminating the action before the defendant has been placed in jeopardy or where the defendant has waived jeopardy. If, pursuant to this subdivision, the people prosecute an appeal to decision, or any review of such decision, it shall be binding upon them and they shall be prohibited from refiling the case which was appealed.

Appealable Conditions. The general principle of an appeal is that it is to review an error of law that occurred in the trial or pretrial proceeding. The function of the appellate court is not to review questions of fact. The appellate court relies upon the trier of fact, whether judge or jury, to establish questions of fact. If an error of law has been made, then the appellate court will function to review that error and pass upon it.

Bail. During the appeal, the defendant has no constitutional right to bail. The constitutional guarantee is only applicable before conviction. Penal Code section 1272 provides:

> After conviction of an offense not punishable with death, a defendant who has appealed may be admitted to bail:

1. As a matter of right, when the appeal is from a judgment imposing a fine only
2. As a matter of right, when the appeal is from a judgment imposing imprisonment in cases of misdemeanor.
3. As a matter of discretion in all other cases.

DISMISSALS

Voluntary. The procedure to dismiss an appeal is provided for in Rules on Appeal, number 38, which states:

> An appellant may dismiss his appeal at any time by filing an abandonment thereof, signed by him or his attorney of record. If the record has not yet been filed in the reviewing court, the abandonment shall be filed with the clerk of the superior court, and such filing shall operate to dismiss the appeal and to restore the jurisdiction of the superior court. If the record has been filed in the reviewing court, the abandonment shall be filed in that court, which may order the dismissal and immediate issuance of the remittitur. The clerk of the court in which the abandonment is filed shall immediately notify the adverse party of the filing of the abandonment or the order of dismissal. If the defendant abandons an appeal, the clerk shall notify both the district attorney and the attorney general.

Involuntary. If, during the period of the appeal, the defendant escapes from custody, the court may dismiss his appeal. The court may also dismiss the appeal because it feels there is no basis for it, or upon hearing the arguments thereto, it may decide in favor of the respondent. In the event the court decides in favor of the appellant, the case is reversed and sent back to the trial court for a new trial.

It is a common misconception among police officers that once a defendant's case is won on an appeal he is free from further prosecution. This is not true. The defendant can be tried again for the same offense because a reversal on appeal indicates there was an error at the trial that rendered the court proceedings invalid. A court procedure that was void does not place the defendant in jeopardy, and he cannot, therefore, plead double jeopardy. The defendant may again be tried for the same offense provided the prosecution can prove its case. For example, if the reason for the appeal was evidence which was improperly admitted and the appellate court finds that there was an error of law because of the admittance of such illegal evidence and reverses the conviction, then the prosecution at the second trial may not present such evidence. If such evidence was the basis for the whole case against the defendant, then the prosecution will be unable to proceed at the new trial, and the defendant may never again be tried for that offense.

Appeals, therefore, may result in the ultimate release of the defendant if the prosecutor's entire case rests upon some evidence that the defendant contends was illegally obtained, and, therefore, a reversal of the conviction will, for all practical purposes, amount to a dismissal.

HABEAS CORPUS

A writ of habeas corpus is a procedure that inquires into the lawfulness of restraint or imprisonment of an individual. "Every person unlawfully imprisoned or restrained of his liberty, under any pretense whatever, may prosecute a writ of habeas corpus, to inquire into the cause of such imprisonment or restraint." (C.P.C., sec. 1473)

For example, a person is held incognito while the police question him about a crime he has allegedly committed. The writ will be issued to inquire into the lawfulness of his detention.

Jurisdiction. The jurisdiction to issue a writ of habeas corpus is conferred upon the courts and judges by the California Constitution, article VI, section 10:

The Supreme Court, courts of appeal, superior courts, and their judges have original jurisdiction in habeas corpus proceedings. Those courts also have original jurisdiction in proceedings for extraordinary relief in the nature of mandamus, certiorari, and prohibition.

Superior courts have original jurisdiction in all causes except those given by statute to other trial courts.

The court may make such comment on the evidence and the testimony and credibility of any witness as in its opinion is necessary for the proper determination of the cause.

Illegal Restraint. It is necessary that there be illegal restraint or detention of the defendant before a writ of habeas corpus will be issued. The most flagrant violation of a person's liberty would be to hold him in custody on an unconstitutional statute.

Where a defendant is arrested for a crime he committed and held in jail beyond the time of the statute of limitations, he is being held or detained unlawfully, and a writ of habeas corpus will be issued for his release.

Where a defendant is tried by the Municipal Court for a felony and sentenced to the jail therefor, a writ of habeas corpus will be issued for his release because the Municipal Court had no jurisdiction to try him for a felony.

Where a defendant has been found guilty of a misdemeanor and sentenced to the state prison for six years, he will be released under a writ of habeas corpus because the sentence is improper and illegal.

Unlawful Restraint under Legal Detentions. "Even though a person is legally imprisoned or detained," Fricke writes, "he cannot be subjected to any greater restraint than that authorized by the arrest, commitment, judgment or order by virtue of which he is being detained, nor can he while under such detention or imprisonment be deprived or denied of such rights as are his under the law. Thus, where a person has been committed to jail for a contempt by an order which includes the provision that while in confinement he shall do hard labor, the court will on habeas corpus order that he be discharged from that portion of his detention which includes the performance of labor but, since the order for detention is otherwise valid, he will be remanded to jail for legal detention." *

For example, if a defendant is sentenced to imprisonment for life for counterfeiting, he may be released because the maximum sentence for such an offense is one to fourteen years.

Petition. Penal Code section 1475 provides:
> Application for the writ is made by petition, signed either by the party for whose relief it is intended, or by some person in his behalf, and must specify:
> 1. That the person in whose behalf the writ is applied for is imprisoned or restrained of his liberty, the officer or person by whom he is so confined or restrained, and the place where, naming all the parties, if they are known, or describing them, if they are not known;
> 2. If the imprisonment is alleged to be illegal, the petition must also state in what the alleged illegality consists;
> 3. The petition must be verified by the oath or affirmation of the party making the application.

Form and Contents of Application. Penal Code section 1475, paragraph 2, requires that "Every application for a writ of habeas corpus must be verified, and shall state whether any prior application or applications have been made for a writ in regard to the same detention or restraint complained of in the application, and if any such prior application or applications have been made the later application must contain a brief statement of all proceedings had therein, or in any of them, to and including the final order or orders made therein, or in any of them, on appeal or otherwise."

Service of Copy of Application. Section 1475, paragraph 3, of the Penal Code states: "Whenever the person applying for a writ of

---

* Charles W. Fricke, *California Criminal Procedure*, 6th ed., Legal Book Store, Los Angeles, 1962, p. 569.

habeas corpus is held in custody or restraint by any officer of any court of this State or any political subdivision thereof, or by any peace officer of this State, or any political subdivision thereof, a copy of the application for such writ must in all cases be served upon the district attorney of the county wherein such person is held in custody or restraint at least 24 hours before the time at which said writ is made returnable and no application for such writ can be heard without proof of such service in cases where such service is required."

Direction. "The writ," states Penal Code section 1477, "must be directed to the person having custody of or restraining the person on whose behalf the application is made, and must command him to have the body of such person before the court or judge before whom the writ is returnable, at a time and place therein specified."

Return. Penal Code section 1480 makes these stipulations:

> The person upon whom the writ is served must state in his return, plainly and unequivocally:
> 1. Whether he has or has not the party in his custody, or under his power or restraint;
> 2. If he has the party in his custody or power, or under his restraint, he must state the authority and cause of such imprisonment or restraint;
> 3. If the party is detained by virtue of any writ, warrant, or other written authority, a copy thereof must be annexed to the return, and the original produced and exhibited to the court or judge on the hearing of such return;
> 4. If the person upon whom the writ is served had a party in his power or custody, or under his restraint, at any time prior or subsequent to the date of the writ of habeas corpus, but has transferred such custody or restraint to another, the return must state particularly to whom, at what time and place, for what cause, and by what authority such transfer took place;

5. The return must be signed by the person making the same, and, except when such person is a sworn public officer, and makes such return in his official capacity, it must be verified by his oath.

Body Produced. "The person to whom the writ is directed, if it is served, must bring the body of the party in his custody or under his restraint, according to the command of the writ, except in the cases specified in the next section." (C.P.C., sec. 1481)

Exceptions. Penal Code section 1482 specifies this exception: "When, from sickness or infirmity of the person directed to be produced, he cannot, without danger, be brought before the court or judge, the person in whose custody or power he is may state that fact in his return to the writ, verifying the same by affidavit. If the court or judge is satisfied of the truth of such return, and the return to the writ is otherwise sufficient, the court or judge may proceed to decide on such return, and to dispose of the matter as if such party had been produced on the writ, or the hearing thereof may be adjourned until such party can be produced."

Hearing. "The court or judge before whom the writ is returned must, immediately after the return, proceed to hear and examine the return, and such other matters as may be properly submitted to their hearing and consideration." (C.P.C., sec. 1483)

Penal Code section 1484 states further:

> The party brought before the court or judge, on the return of the writ, may deny or controvert any of the material facts or matters set forth in the return, or except to the sufficiency thereof, or allege any fact to show either that his imprisonment or detention is unlawful, or that he is entitled to his discharge. The court or judge must thereupon proceed in a summary way to hear such proof as may be produced against such imprisonment or detention, or in favor of the same, and to dis-

pose of such party as the justice of the case may require, and have full power and authority to require and compel the attendance of witnesses, by process of subpoena and attachment, and to do and perform all other acts and things necessary to a full and fair hearing and determination of the case.

Discharge or Removal to Custody. If the court concludes after the hearing that the party has been illegally detained or imprisoned, the party is discharged from custody. If the court determines that the party has been legally detained or imprisoned, it will remand him to the custody of the person entrusted with his imprisonment.

SUMMARY

A writ of coram nobis is used to set aside a plea of guilty on the basis that fraud, duress, coercion, or mistake existed that induced the plea. A motion for a new trial is a motion for reexamination of the issue in the same court before another judge or jury.

A demurrer is a pleading that attacks the sufficiency of the accusatory pleading.

All procedures for appealing cases are set forth in statutes. The procedures must be strictly complied with or the defendant waives his appeal rights.

A writ of habeas corpus is a procedure that inquires into the lawfulness of restraint or imprisonment of an individual.

QUESTIONS

1. What is a writ of coram nobis? Is there any statutory basis for such a motion?
2. What is the common basis for such a motion?
3. What is a motion to set aside judgment? When is it made?
4. Name the grounds for a motion for new trial.

5. What is a demurrer and how is it used in a civil proceeding? In a criminal proceeding?
6. To what court is an appeal made from a Municipal Court trial?
7. Under what circumstances may the people appeal?
8. When is bail a matter of right?
9. Under what circumstances is a writ of habeas corpus granted?
10. What is meant by "illegal restraint" in a writ of habeas corpus?
11. What is meant by "producing the body"?

glossary

Accusatory pleading
a complaint, indictment, or information charging a person with a public offense

Accused
a defendant in a criminal trial

Admission
an acknowledgment of the existence of a fact; not to be confused with the term "confession" (see below)

Affidavit
a written declaration, made under oath, to an adverse party

Affirmation
used in lieu of a legal oath, but still a promise to tell the truth in a criminal trial

Allegation
that which a party expects to prove in a legal action; part of a pleading

Appellate court
a court having the jurisdiction of review and appeal

Arraignment
the bringing of a criminal defendant before the court to answer a criminal charge

Attest
to affirm to be true

Attorney
a counsel or advocate who represents persons in court

Bail
a procedure whereby a person who has been arrested may be released from custody after depositing a sum of money to ensure his presence in court for further proceeding

Bailiff
a police officer assigned to preserve peace in the courtroom

Bench
refers to the judge's desk in the courtroom, as in "take the issue before the bench"

Bench warrant
a legal process issued by a magistrate for the purpose of arrest or for bringing before the court a witness who does not honor a subpoena

Capital case
one in which the punishment is death

Certiorari
a writ issued from a higher court to an inferior court directing that a pending proceeding, or records thereof, be sent up for review

Change of venue
the removal of an action from one jurisdiction to another; usually in regard to ensuring a fair trial

Civil proceeding
an action where money damages or a court order directing or restricting a certain action is sought

Code of civil procedure
the state statutes that prescribe procedure in civil actions

Commitment
the legal act of imprisonment by a court by means of an order or warrant

Common law
the unwritten law of England upon which American law is largely based; case law is used by this reference in opposition to statutory law

Complaint
a pleading used to charge a person with a crime

Confession
a complete acknowledgment of guilt regarding the commission of a crime

Coram nobis
a procedure whereby a party petitions the court that rendered a judgment adverse to him to review a mistake of *fact* at the trial

Coroner's jury
a jury called to investigate the cause of death

Corpus delicti
the essential elements of any given crime

Court
a judicial tribunal

Court clerk
the secretary to the judge

Court trial
a trial before a judge

Crime
an act or omission of an act in violation of the penal laws of the state; usually regarded as an offense against the state

Criminal proceeding
an action wherein the remedy sought is punishment

Defendant
the person against whom relief is sought in a court proceeding

Degree of proof
the amount of proof needed for a judgment

Demurrer
a pleading that attacks the sufficiency of the accusation

Deposition
a question and answer proceeding taken under oath before a court reporter

Duces tecum
a writ commonly called "subpoena duces tecum" which requires a subpoenaed party to bring a specific document or article of evidence before the court

Escheat
the return of land to the state

Evidence
the means sanctioned by law of ascertaining a fact in a judicial proceeding; the truth respecting a question of fact

Ex parte
on one side only; by or for one party; done for, in behalf of, or on the application of, one party only (*Black's Law Dictionary*, 4th ed.)

Extradition
the act of a state surrendering a person within its jurisdiction to another state

Felony
a serious offense, one punishable by imprisonment in the state prison or by death

General verdict
the decision of the jury as to either acquittal or conviction

Grand jury
the investigative body of the community

Indictment
a pleading used by the grand jury to charge a person with a crime

Information
a pleading used by the district attorney to charge a person with a crime

Inquest
an inquiry into a sudden, violent, or otherwise unusual death; usually termed a "coroner's inquest"

Insanity
the state of being insane; a mental capability so impaired as to prevent a person from comprehending the nature and consequences of his acts; legally, being unable to distinguish between right and wrong

Jurisdiction
the power to hear and decide certain types of cases

Jury trial
a trial before a jury

Magistrate
an officer of the court empowered to issue warrants; usually a judge

Magna Carta
(Great Charter) an agreement signed by King John of England on June 15, 1215, granting certain rights to his barons; also included certain rights of the freemen as granted by the barons; called the "cornerstone of English Liberty" regarded as the basis for democratic society

Mala in se
wrongs which are wrong within themselves; usually moral offenses against the conscience

Malum prohibitum
a wrong prohibited by society; usually in the form of statutory law

Malum in se
a wrong in itself (see "mala in se," above)

Mens rea
a guilty mind; the state of criminal intent

Misdemeanor
a minor offense, one punishable by not more than one year in the county jail

Nolle prosequi
a formal entry upon the record, by . . . the prosecuting officer in a criminal action, by which he declares that he "will no further prosecute" the case, either as to some of the counts, or some of the defendants, or altogether (*Black's Law Dictionary*, 4th ed.)

Nolo contendere
a plea stating no contest

Objection
a procedure whereby evidence is questioned during a trial

Once in jeopardy
a phrase used to express the condition of a person charged with crime, who has once already, by legal proceedings, been put in danger of conviction and punishment for the same offense (*Black's Law Dictionary*, 4th ed.)

Opening statement
the statement made at the outset of a trial advising the court or jury of the prosecution's or defense's case

Peremptory challenge
a challenge to a juror for which no reason need be given

Plaintiff
the moving party in a court proceeding

Preliminary examination
a proceeding to determine whether there is reasonable cause to believe a public offense has been committed

Prosecutor
an attorney employed by the state or county to prosecute persons for crimes; usually the district attorney

Public defender
an attorney paid by the county to defend indigent persons accused of committing a crime

Special verdict
a decision of jury as to *facts* only

Stare decisis
a legal doctrine that refers to the standing of decided cases until such case decision is changed through legal process

Statute of limitations
the statutory time within which a person may be prosecuted or a civil action filed

Subpoena
a court order compelling witnesses to appear in court (see "duces tecum," above)

Summons
a writ directed to a peace officer which requires the notification of a person named as defendant in an action, stipulating the day and time he is required to appear to answer the charges

Surety
the person who deposits the funds for bail with the court

Venue
the place of trial

Verdict
the decision of the jury

Waiver of time
an action whereby the defendant waives his right to a speedy trial

Writ of habeas corpus
a procedure that inquires into the lawfulness of restraint or imprisonment of an individual

index

Admonishment, 185–186
Answer, held to, 81
Antitrust actions, 30
Appeal(s):
  automatic, 146
  bail during, 203–204
  conditions of, 203
  by defendant, 201
  from inferior courts, 202
  by the people, 202–203
  procedure, 202
  from superior courts, 202
Argument, final, 102
  contents of, 103
  procedure of, 103
Arraignments, 37, 54
Arrest(s):
  citizen's, 179–180
  defendant's rights during, 184–186
  duties of peace officer, 182–186
  forcible entry, 182–184
  by peace officer, 175–178
  by warrant, 169–175
  without warrant, 169–175
Assize of Clarendon, 6

Bail, 189–194
  forfeiture of, 193

Bankruptcy, 30

Capital punishment, 144–147
Cause:
  probable, 180–182
  reasonable, 180–182
  sufficient, 80
Challenges, 86
  for cause, 86
  exercise of, 91
  number of, 91
  peremptory, 86
Citizenship matters, 30
Commitment, 81
Complaints, 52
Constitution:
  California State, 16
  United States, 15
Continuances, 70, 71
Copyrights, 30
Council, Judicial, 17, 47
Counsel, right to, 58, 184–185
Court(s), 12
  appellate, 31, 201
    District Court of Appeal, 33, 34
  jurisdiction of, 28
  term of justices for, 17

219

Court(s):
  of claims, 30
  customs, 30
  federal, 14
    system for, 27
  justice, 38
  local, 32
  municipal, 32, 37
    jurisdiction of: exclusive, 37
      in misdemeanor cases, 37
    officers of, 45
    sessions, 44
      location of, 44
      time of, 45.
  state, 14
    California State Supreme Court, 33
    supreme, 31
    system for, 31
  superior, 34
    departments of, 35
    judges, 17
    trial, 35
  United States Circuit Court of Appeals, 29
  United States District Courts, 29
  United States Supreme Court, 28
Criminals, habitual, 141–144

Defendants, 20
  presence of, 9–10, 55
Demurrer, 199–201
Discharge, 79
Dismissals:
  automatic, 66
  for felonies, 72
  involuntary, 204–205
  for misdemeanors, 71
  voluntary, 204

Electorate, 16
Evidence, 100–101, 165
Examination, direct, 100
  (See also Preliminary examination)
Execution, 144–147
  waiver of, 189

Grand jury (see Juries, grand)

Habeas corpus, 205
  discharge or removal to custody, 210
  form and content of, 207
  hearing, 209
  illegal restraint before, 206
  jurisdiction for, 205–206
  petition for, 207
  return of, 208
  service of application for, 207
  unlawful restraint before, 206–207
Habitual criminals, 141–144
Hammurabic Code, 3

Indictments, 52
Information, 52
Insanity, 115
  burden of proof of, 67
  Durham rule on, 68
  before execution, 69
  M'Naghten rule for determination of, 67–68
  present, 68
  procedure for plea of, 67
  test for, 67
  during trial, 68

Judgment, motion to set aside, 198
Judicial Council, 17, 47
Juries, 23
  coroner's, 24
  grand, 24, 38
    books of county officials examined by, 42
    duties of jurors on, 41
    examination of officials, 41
    immunity of jurors on, 41
    lands subject to escheat proceedings by, 43
    public sessions of, 44
    secrecy of proceedings of, 40
Jurisdiction, 14
  appellate, 28
  concurrent, 30
  discretionary, 29
  exclusive, 14
  limited, 32
Jurors:
  bias of, 90
  qualifications of, 84–85

index

Jury:
   deliberation by, 107
   instructions to, 104
      erroneous, 106
      procedure and content of, 104
      rereading of, 106
   selection of, 85
   swearing in of, 92

Law:
   Assyrian, 2
   English, 5–6
   English common, 7
   French, 5
   Greek, 4
   of Moses, 4
   Roman, 4–5

Magna Carta, 7, 38
Miranda warning, 185–186
Misdemeanors, procedure for, 55
Motion(s):
   for new trial, 198
      effect of granting, 199
      procedure for, 199
   to set aside judgment, 198

Notes, use on witness stand of, 166

Objections, 99–100
Offenders, sex (*see* Sexual psychopath)
Offenses, nonbailable, 192

Past recollections refreshed, 166
Plaintiff, 20
Pleading, 51–53
Pleas, 57
   former judgment of conviction or acquittal, 57
   guilty, 57, 76
   nolo contendere, 58
   not guilty, 57
      by reason of insanity, 58
   once in jeopardy, 57
Prejudicial conduct, 119
Preliminary examination, 75

Preliminary examination:
   of defendant, 78
   exclusion of public from, 79
   postponement of, 77
   presence of defendant at, 77
   procedure for, 77
   purposes of, 76
   reading of depositions of witnesses at, 77
   waiver of, 76
   of witnesses, 78
Probation:
   basic law governing, 149–153
   conditions of, 154–156
   officers, 114–115
Proceedings:
   civil, 19
   criminal, 19, 21, 22

Release on own recognizance, 193–194
Right(s):
   to counsel, 58, 184–185
   to remain silent, 185–186

Sentences:
   concurrent, 140–141
   consecutive, 140–141
   death, 144–147
   indeterminate, 138–139
Sexual psychopath, 120–131
Silent, right to remain, 185–186
Statute of limitations, 59
   if defendant is out of state, 61
   for felonies, 60
   when lesser included offenses are involved, 61
   for misdemeanors, 60

Time, waiver of, 66
Trial(s), 83
   by combat, 6
   by compurgation, 6
   court, 22
   criminal, 36
   defense counsel's role during, 95, 96
   district attorney's role during, 92, 93

Trial(s):
  jury, 22
  opening statement of, 99
  by ordeal, 6
  order of, 83
  procedure, 92
  prosecutor's role during, 92
  public defender's role during, 97
  speedy, importance of, 65

United States Code Annotated, 29
  [*See also* Court(s)]
United States Constitution, 15
  [*See also* Court(s)]
United States vessels, suits involving, 30
  [*See also* Court(s)]

Venue, change of, 69–70
Verdict(s), 108
  degree of crime determined for rendering of, 109

Verdict(s):
  general, 109
  previous offenses determined for rendering of, 109
  recommendations of the court on, 110
  special, 109
  types of, 109
  when lesser offenses and attempts are included, 110
  when two or more defendants are charged, 110
Vessels (*see* United States vessels)
Vicecomes, 6

Waiver of time, 66
Warrants:
  felony, 169–173
  misdemeanor, 173–175
  out-of-town, 174–175
Writ(s):
  of certiorari, 29
  of coram nobis, 197